11+ ENGLISH
REVISION GUIDE

Susan Hamlyn

9 40177543

Published by Galore Park Publishing Ltd
An Hachette UK Company, Carmelite House, 50 Victoria Embankment, London,
EC4Y 0DZ
www.galorepark.co.uk

Cover design by Helen Boosey
Design and layout by Qué, Wittersham

Printed and bound in the UK by Ashford Colour Press Ltd, Gosport, Hampshire

ISBN 978 1 905735 587

First published 2012, 2013, Reprinted 2015

Details of other Galore Park publications are available at www.galorepark.co.uk

The publishers are grateful to the following for permission to use the extracts
included in this book:
Emil and the Detectives by Erich Kastner is reproduced with permission of Curtis
Brown Group Ltd, London on behalf of the Estate of Erich Kastner. Copyright © the
Estate of Erich Kastner, 1929; article from the *National Trust Magazine* Summer 1998
(permission sought); 'Gathering Leaves' by Robert Frost from *The Poetry of Robert
Frost* edited by Edward Connery Latham. Published by Jonathon Cape. Reprinted by
permission of The Random House Group Limited; extract from *The Hamlyn Book of
Dinosaurs* by Michael Benton (permission sought); 'She lies by the Island of Spices
and Zephyrs' by George Barker from *To Aylsham Fair*, published by Faber and Faber
Ltd; *My Family and Other Animals* by Gerald Durrell. Reproduced with permission of
Curtis Brown Group Ltd, London on behalf of the Estate of Gerald Durrell.
Copyright © the Estate of Gerald Durrell, 1956; extract adapted from *The Atlas of
Holy Places and Sacred Sites* by Colin Wilson published by Dorling Kindersley in 1996
(permission sought); from *The Silver Sword* by Ian Serraillier. Published by Jonathon
Cape. Reprinted by permission of The Random House Group Limited; from *Winter
Tales* by George Mackay Brown (permission sought); article abridged and adapted
from *National Trust News*, December 2010, reproduced with permission of the
National Trust.

Every effort has been made to trace the copyright holders of extracts used in this
publication and any outstanding information will be included here at the next
available opportunity.

For Colin Carter

Acknowledgements

Thanks are due for help and test piloting many of the exercises, which first appeared in my book *11+ English: A Parent's Toolkit* (published by *The Good Schools Guide*), to The King's School Rochester Preparatory School and their Head Master, Roger Overend. Thanks to the many – too many to name – children who have helped me evolve the practices and techniques in this book over many enjoyable and productive years. Special thanks to James Combe, Alisha Godhania, Ali Moodie and Asha Sandhu for giving up a day's summer holiday to trial some new exercises and eat biscuits. And Edward Higgins who did it on his own. Thanks to St Paul's Girls' School, London for rights to reproduce an adapted version of their comprehension questions on George Mackay Brown's *Winter Tales*. Thanks to my family for putting up with the way I bash the keyboard.

CONTENTS

INTRODUCTION

This book has been written to help you revise and to help you improve your English skills. You can use it to focus on things you find tricky and you can ignore it when it tells you things you feel confident about. It gives you advice on how to:

- spell
- punctuate
- avoid common mistakes
- write good essays – to a time limit
- answer comprehension questions.

You can use this book on your own, or a parent (or other adult) can work through it with you. It should be fun and useful – never boring or frustrating. You can be joint learners. But only you have to take the exam. So make sure it's you who does the work.

About this book

This book is designed to be used for all 11+ examinations and is in three main parts:

1. **The rules of writing** concentrates on spelling, punctuation and grammar and how to avoid common mistakes in these areas.
2. **Improving your writing skills** focuses on making writing appropriate, clear and interesting in preparation for the exam.
3. **The exam** looks at the two components of most English exams: a comprehension and an essay and how to tackle these. It then provides practice comprehension exercises with related essay questions.

Throughout the book you will find: **to do** boxes containing practice exercises; **top tips** which are helpful reminders and snippets of advice and **aim high** material to help stretch and develop skills further.

Answers to the exercises that appear throughout the book and to the comprehension questions are, where appropriate, at the back of the book.

A note for teachers

This book covers all the skills and techniques needed to develop confidence and proficiency in English. It is lively, collaborative and fun. It is packed with practical advice. All 9–11 year olds – whatever their ability – will find their English skills improve if they make good use of this book.

A note for parents

This book has been written primarily to assist the increasing number of parents who wish to support their children in preparation for the important assessment and selection process at 11+. It will help you diagnose and then work on those aspects of your child's English that need attention. It should also help to make all aspects of English work enjoyable.

Past papers (including ISEB Common Entrance papers available from Galore Park) can be used to provide invaluable practice but practice is not enough. It helps children to build up speed but doesn't actually help them revise in the way this book is designed to do.

What else do we need?

Alongside this book, your child will need the following:
- a standard A5 **exercise book** – ideally wide-lined with a margin.
- the correct writing implement – some schools like children to use a **fountain pen** and an ink eraser while others prefer a **pencil** and rubber. The two most important factors for children are comfort and the legibility of their writing.

- a collection of **postcards** as triggers for story writing – include landscapes, street scenes, people, abstracts, jokey pictures, etc. You can also use pictures from the front of greetings cards, magazines, etc.

- a **dictionary** – all children should have their own portable dictionary; you might want to invest in a big one for the whole family to use.

- a **spelling book** – a plain address book with indexed pages – at least one page for each letter. This becomes your child's personal dictionary (see page 5 for more details).

- **patience and praise** – these are your most important tools. A happy child who is made to feel clever will outperform an anxious one every time.

When and where should we work?

Check when your child will be taking the exam(s) and make a start on revising about a year beforehand. If your child has few problems with English and just needs practice and to build up speed, this should allow you to progress in a relaxed and comfortable manner. If, however, you have identified problems with essay writing or with basics such as spelling, punctuation or reading carefully, you may well want to begin earlier.

Lessons should be strictly time-limited to an hour. Choose a regular time when neither you nor your child is too tired and when you don't want or need to be doing something else. You may find that first thing in the morning at a weekend or before the evening meal is a good time for you both.

Decide on a place to work together. The kitchen table is fine. Wherever you are, make sure that the TV is off and interruptions are minimised.

How to use this book

It makes sense to start with an assessment of how your child tackles comprehension exercises and essay writing. This will enable you to identify any particular problems. You can then concentrate on those parts of this book that will help your child and leave those aspects that need less work.

Start by asking your child to read aloud one of the comprehension passages in this book – see page 56 for a relatively easy one. Then ask your child to try the questions that follow the passage. Now ask your child the following questions to see how they got on:

- Did you find the questions easy or difficult?
- Did you find it easy to put answers into your own words – clearly and simply – or did you feel you knew what the answer was but found it hard to explain?
- Did you answer all the questions in the time given?

This will give you an idea of how good your child is at comprehensions and how much time and effort will be required for your child to feel confident. There are lots of tips and suggestions on how to approach comprehensions on pages 38–41. You should also look through the rest of the book to identify those areas where you can see that your child needs some more help.

Then give your child an essay title from the list on page 45 (or a limited choice of titles from this list). Allow half an hour for thinking and writing and a further five minutes for checking. This should enable you to assess whether your child:

- can write a connected narrative or description
- has a sense of writing something *for a reader*, i.e. that a reader can follow and make sense of
- can punctuate competently
- can spell most words accurately
- can write in an interesting way and use words in a confident, lively and imaginative way
- can write for half an hour and understand what can – and can't – be done in that time
- can check work effectively.

This should help you to point your child towards the parts of the book that will be of most use.

Tips on revising

It is suggested that you should:

- get physical exercise, such as going for a walk, before revising
- eat healthy food, such as fresh fruit, whilst revising
- appreciate that you know, understand and can do a great deal already, so keep calm and don't worry
- set yourself a realistic target, such as concentrating just on spelling
- work for a short time, such as fifteen minutes, and then take a break before continuing
- have a good night's sleep.

Tips on the final preparation for an exam

You will have worked on past papers so you will know roughly what to expect with the examination paper.

You will already have some experience of examinations, so you know what it feels like. We are all different, but most people will be apprehensive.

Assuming that you have worked hard in class and you have revised thoroughly, you will be in a good position to do your best.

It is suggested that you:

- make sure you have everything you need, such as pens and pencils, checked and ready in good time (at the latest, the day before)
- get a good night's sleep so you can think clearly in the exam
- eat a sensible breakfast so you do not feel hungry during the exam
- resist the temptation to do any last minute revision
- keep calm
- take a small bottle of water into the exam, if this is allowed
- make sure that you go to the lavatory and wash your hands before you enter the exam room.

Avoid:

- leaving everything until the last minute
- rushing about, getting hot and sweaty
- doing anything which might affect your eyes, such as going for a swim or giving the cat a hug!

Tips on what to do in an exam

It is suggested that you:

- listen to, and read, all instructions very carefully
- read each question very carefully, remembering that a single word, such as 'not', can change a question considerably
- work as quickly and as neatly as you can
- check that your answers are sensible and complete
- don't worry, or spend a lot of time, if there is something you find particularly difficult – just leave it and come back to it after you have done everything else.

USEFUL RESOURCES

From the same series *11+ Maths Revision Guide* by David E Hanson, ISBN 9781905735761

Study Skills by Elizabeth Holtom, ISBN 9781902984599

English Practice Exercises 11+ by Andrew Hammond, ISBN 9780903627696
English Practice Exercises 11+ Answer Book by Andrew Hammond, ISBN 9781907047848

Junior English Book 1 by Andrew Hammond, ISBN 9781902984827
Junior English Book 1 Answer Book by Andrew Hammond, ISBN 9781902984872
Junior English Book 2 by Andrew Hammond, ISBN 9781902984810
Junior English Book 2 Answer Book by Andrew Hammond, ISBN 9781902984865
Junior English Book 3 by Andrew Hammond, ISBN 9781902984803
Junior English Book 3 Answer Book by Andrew Hammond, ISBN 9781902984858

So you really want to learn English Book 1 (2nd edition) by Susan Elkin, ISBN 9781905735518
So you really want to learn English Book 1 Answer Book (2nd edition) by Susan Elkin,
ISBN 9781905735648
So you really want to learn English Book 2 (2nd edition) by Susan Elkin, ISBN 9781905735624
So you really want to learn English Book 2 Answer Book (2nd edition) by Susan Elkin,
ISBN 9781905735686

Galore Park is sole distributor of the Independent Schools Examinations Board (ISEB) past papers for Common Entrance examinations and Common Academic Scholarship Examinations

All this plus much more available from Galore Park: www.galorepark.co.uk

1 THE RULES OF WRITING

This chapter focuses on the rules of writing by looking at the importance of spelling words correctly, punctuating properly and using grammar accurately, with plenty of practice to ensure you are confident in all three areas.

SPELLING

Some people **spell** and **punctuate** correctly without needing to think about it! Is this you?

Do you always remember to add an -ly when you want to turn 'final' into 'finally'? And are there one or two words you can *never* remember how to spell?

Learning lists of words has *some* value but usually only if they are words you know and use. Copying out a word a dozen times or more can also help to stick it in your head. You may have been taught the 'study – cover – copy' technique or other helpful tricks.

It is very useful to make your own **spelling book**. You will need a plain address book with indexed pages – at least one page for each letter – and preferably no special spaces for telephone numbers, email addresses and so on.

Whenever you misspell a word or if you meet a new word and want to learn it or if you are given words to learn, write them into your spelling book. You will build up your own personal dictionary. Ideally, each time you write in a new word, you should spend a minute looking over the words already on that page.

TOP TIP

Do you find that you sometimes copy a word wrongly? If so, try copying the word in groups of three letters at a time. For example, when copying out 'necessary', study the first three letters 'nec' and hold them in your head while covering the word and copying them out. Then do the same with 'ess' and finish with 'ary'.

TOP TIP

Your spelling book is your own personal dictionary. Use it at home and at school.

Spelling list

Here is a list taken from the spelling books of other children your age. Do you know how to spell all of these words? They are all common words you may well use, so try to learn any you don't know.

absolutely	accident	actually
another	answered	article
August	author	a lot (it is *two* words)
beautiful	beginning	believe
biscuit	business	ceiling
certain	chief	choose
colour	completely	concentration
concrete	dangerous	deceive
decided	decision	definitely
delicious	desperate	different
disappearance	disappeared	disappoint
discussed	edge	eight
embarrassed	especially	excited
extremely	favourite	February
figure	finally	friend

To do

Here are ten of the most commonly misspelled words: beginning, business, decision, definite, embarrassing, excited, imagine, interesting, properly, surprise.

To do

Here are ten more commonly misspelled words: absolutely, article, author, disappeared, discussed, necessary, occasion, recognise, remember, separate.

gadget	giant	guard
guide	guitar	horrible
hour	imagine	immediately
important	interested	interesting
January	jealous	juice
laughter	library	listened
lose	machine	majesty
measure	minute	mountain
natural	necessary	no-one
normally	nuisance	occasion
opportunity	orchestra	parallel
parents	peculiar	people
piece	position	prejudice
probably	profession	professor
pronunciation	properly	receive
recognise	remember	sausage
scared	separate	several
sincerely	straight	strength
successful	superstitious	sure
surprise	suspicious	system
terrified	thought	through
tomorrow	tongue	tragedy
tunnel	until	unusual
usually	Wednesday	weight
which	wizard	

To do

Look at the commonly misspelled words in the boxes on page 5 or identify ten of the words in the spelling list that you know you find difficult. Get your parent or another adult to ask you to spell them aloud. If you get one wrong, spell it out loud until you get it right. Then write two sentences for each word you got wrong.

Common spelling confusions

Adding -ly

Some people have no problem with these two little letters. But if you do – read on!

The **suffix** '-ly' is added to an **adjective** to make an **adverb**, for example, sad becomes sadly.

Here are some tips:

● For words that end in 'y', the 'y' changes to an 'i', for example, happy becomes happ*ily*.

TOP TIP
A suffix is a letter or group of letters added to the end of a word to make a new word.

To do

Change the following adjectives into adverbs: pretty, sunny, dozy, crazy, funny, cosy, gloomy, shiny.
Make some sentences or a story using the words you have made.

● Words that end in 'l' do *not* lose their existing 'l', so they have two 'l's, for example, final and normal become fina*lly* and norma*lly*.

To do

Change the following adjectives into adverbs: actual, formal, hopeful. Make some sentences or a story using the words you have made.

TOP TIP
Words that end in -ful always have a double 'l' when they change to ending in -fully, for example, helpful and beautiful become helpfully and beautifully.

● Words that end in 'e' do not – in general – drop the final 'e', for example, extreme and wise become extreme*ly* and wise*ly*.

 Change the following adjectives into adverbs: close, brave, remote.
Make some sentences or a story using the words you have made.

There are some exceptions. Some words that end in -ble, -mble, -tle, -ple or -kle *do* lose the 'e'.

For example:	
nimble	nimbly
capable	capably
amiable	amiably
sensible	sensibly
humble	humbly
gentle	gently
simple	simply
sparkle	sparkly

TOP TIP
Put these exceptions in your spelling book and learn them separately.

Words ending in '-ue' also lose the final 'e', for example, due and true become du*ly* and tru*ly*.

Add '-ly' to the following words and put them into sentences of your own: casual, safe, factual, practical, wise, polite, helpful, total, thankful, special, natural, brave, thoughtful, typical, doubtful, usual, cheerful, aggressive, extreme, final.

Adding 'd' or -ed

To put a **regular verb** into the **past tense**, add 'd' or '-ed'.

● For verbs that already end in 'e' only add a 'd', for example, save and cope become save*d* and cope*d*.

● For verbs that end in 'y' with a consonant before the 'y', turn the 'y' into an 'i' and add '-ed', for example, copy and try become cop*ied* and tr*ied*.

● For some verbs you need to double the last consonant before adding '-ed', for example, bat and hum become bat*ted* and hum*med*.

Turn all these words into the past tense by adding 'd' or '-ed':

joke	flatter	sniff
climb	hurry	smile
thrill	surprise	tramp
tame	spot	battle
adopt	snap	spy
cuddle	like	act

TOP TIP
Sometimes the '-ed' sounds more like a 't', as in 'smoked', which can be confusing. Underline the words where you actually hear the '-ed' sound when you say the word.

 Put these sentences into the past tense:
● Sarah and Laura (pour) the popcorn into a bowl and (start) to munch.
● Karim and Naveen (cycle) to the park and (wave) to some friends.
● Mrs Chinwicket (stir) the pot after she (skin) the slippery snake.
● Mr Morpish (marry) Miss Chirping after they (learn) to dance at an evening class.
● Laura (copy) Karim's homework but Mrs Chinwicket (spot) it.

Double letters

Adding '-ing' to a word can often be treated in the same way as adding '-ed'. For example, stop becomes stopped/stopping and chat becomes chatted/chatting.

Here are some examples, using the '-ed' suffix:

stab	stabbed	hum	hummed
bob	bobbed	fan	fanned
rub	rubbed	bin	binned
rig	rigged	stun	stunned
lag	lagged	rap	rapped
chug	chugged	drip	dripped
fulfil	fulfilled	shop	shopped
instil	instilled	bat	batted
rebel	rebelled	knit	knitted
ram	rammed	jut	jutted
dim	dimmed		

TOP TIP
Words that double their final letter like this almost all end in b, g, l, m, n, p or t.

TOP TIP
To add '-ing' to any of these words, double the final letter in exactly the same way.

You can see how important this is by looking at the following words:

- hop + -ing without the double 'p' becomes hoping not hopping
- tap becomes taping not tapping
- sham becomes shaming not shamming.
  (Shamming means falsely presenting something as the truth.)

To do

Add '-ing' or '-ed' to the following words, remembering to double the final letter first:

trip	strap
slip	slim
flop	skip
bat	thin

To do

In the following sentences, put the words in brackets into the past tense:

- Sarah and Laura (chop) firewood for the bonfire and (drop) a lighted match to start it off.
- Mr Morpish (scrap) his car last week.
- Julia (scar) herself with the rusty nail.

TOP TIP
Think about the last two example words. What difference does it make if you don't double the last letter?

Remember that you never have double letters after:

- double vowels: ai, ea, ee, oa, oo, oi, ui, ue
- after long single vowels: 'a' pronounced 'ay', 'e' pronounced 'ee', 'i' pronounced 'eye', 'o' pronounced 'oh' or 'u' pronounced 'you'.

Words ending in -ous or -ious

Lots of words end with these groups of letters. Note that a 'c' or a 't' in front of the -ious makes a 'sh' sound, for example cau*tious*, suspi*cious*. If you struggle with these, just learn and practise them. Here is a list of words with these endings that you may come across most often:

-ous	**-ious**
nervous	malicious
anonymous	cautious
glamorous	amphibious
barbarous	ambitious
bulbous	delicious
fabulous	religious
gluttonous	laborious
arduous	precious
scandalous	curious
horrendous	suspicious
porous	superstitious
timorous	anxious
disastrous	luxurious

TOP TIP

The 'sh' sound found in many of the -ious words listed is also found in words that end in -tion or -ssion, for example caution, action, passion, session. Make a list of as many of these words as you can think of.

There are also a few words that end in -eous, for example gorgeous, hideous, righteous.

Words ending in -ough

This is the oddest and trickiest group of words in all English spelling. In fact, there are eight different ways in which this group of four letters can be pronounced!

1. cough
   trough

2. enough
   tough
   rough

3. though
   although

4. through

5. thorough
   borough

6. Slough

7. brought
   bought
   ought
   thought

8. lough

TOP TIP

'Lough' is another way of spelling 'loch' and is pronounced in the same way.

To do

You just have to learn these, so concentrate on the ones that you find difficult and write them in your spelling book.

Word games

Word games are fun and a great way to practise spelling without it feeling like work. Try some of the following:

- Scrabble® – play the junior version to start with if you like
- anagram games – make a word from the letters of another word, for example 'bleat' from the letters in 'table'
- Hangman
- take a nine-letter word and make other words from it. Start small and make bigger words. For example, the word 'playground' has three-letter words: pal, lay, pay, dog, lap; four-letter words: gulp, pray, drop, load. You may find even five- or six-letter words
- word searches
- crosswords
- unscrambling – see next page.

TOP TIP

Try Hangman using only words that are, for example, the names of animals, TV programmes, rock groups.

Here are the names of ten foods. How many can you unscramble?

asdal	aspat
zazip	pisch
agussea	rycru
realce	nacob
esheec	chindaws

Here are some more to try. You will find the unscrambled words on page 75.

Animals	**Colours**	**English towns**	**Football clubs**
yemnok	lebu	thrignob	pruss
grite	gorean	noodln	lensara
noli	voteli	desel	cleesha
frigfea	lescrat	roky	stew mah
plateenh	wornb	mudhar	povrileol
droolicce	vyna	tocyvern	snato lival
bartib	nereg	drove	noblot
phese	ewith	nicnoll	seled
flow	yerg	rowchin	auflhm
fabfoul	wolley	slibrot	lubbknarc

Scramble up the names of some of your favourite foods, friends, local shops, countries, colours, means of transport and so on. Give these to your family and friends to unscramble.

TOP TIP

Find other fun games to help improve your spelling and vocabulary.

Computers

You cannot rely on a computer to check your spelling. A spell checker does not know that when you wrote 'leak' you meant to write 'lake'. You can use a computer, however, to play interactive spelling games such as the Times Spelling Bee (www.timesspellingbee.co.uk). Your parents or another adult may be able to find other similar games for you to play on the computer.

PUNCTUATION

Do you know when to use **apostrophes** or do you dangle them hopefully over the end of a word, hoping they are in roughly the right place? Can you set out and **punctuate** a conversation correctly? Do you know where to put **commas**? Do you always remember to start sentences with a **capital letter**? Do you think punctuation doesn't matter?

Look at the following two **sentences** and see what a difference to the meaning punctuation makes:

- The children, who are planning a sleepover, want to buy balloons.
- The children who are planning a sleepover want to buy balloons.

The first sentence indicates that *all* the children are planning the sleepover and want to buy balloons. The second sentence indicates that *only* those children who are planning the sleepover want to buy balloons.

Look at these two sentences:

- The pudding, which took all day to make, was a disaster.
- The pudding which took all day to make was a disaster.

The first sentence indicates that there was only one pudding and it was a disaster. The second one indicates that only one particular pudding out of many took all day to make and was a disaster.

Some people punctuate naturally as they go along without even stopping to think about it. That's great for them. Others need to remind themselves that full stops, commas, capital letters, question marks, exclamation marks, hyphens and speech marks all have their right places.

TOP TIP
The punctuation really does affect the meaning and it matters!

Sentences and paragraphs

A **sentence** is a kind of container – a box – holding one idea. Each new idea needs a new box. However, a box – a sentence – can contain one lesser idea inside the main idea.

> For example:
> - I saw the man who sold me the bike waiting for the bus.
>
>   The main idea in this sentence is:
>
>   > I saw the man waiting for the bus.
>
>   The lesser idea is:
>
>   > The man sold me the bike.

Several boxes of connected ideas need a suitcase – a **paragraph** – to go in. Each paragraph should follow on from the one before and lead naturally to the one after it – a bit like a string of sausages or a series of train carriages.

Commas

As we saw above, **commas** really make a difference and they have a number of particular jobs to do.

Commas:

- Separate items in a list.

  > For example: 'I bought apples, pears, bananas and grapes in the shop.'

- In pairs, go round sections of a sentence which could be taken out and leave the sentence still making sense.

  > For example: 'John, a hard-working father, makes time to help Alice, a clever girl, with her homework'. This sentence still makes sense if you take out the bits between the pairs of commas: 'John makes time to help Alice with her homework.'

- Act as pauses, after a short phrase.

  > For example: 'Washing up, I noticed a crack in my favourite bowl.'

- Are essential in bits of speech that are interrupted by narrative.

  > For example: 'I'm over here,' yelled Rajiv, 'by the compost heap!' They separate the speech from the interrupting narrative and show that the sentence is continuing.

Look at the following passage. You need to split it into two paragraphs and into sentences. Write it out, adding commas (5), full stops (10) and capital letters (15) where appropriate.

sarah has been going to ballet for years every thursday since she was four has been ballet class now she is bored and wants to try something else her friend laura is a brownie but sarah doesnt want to be a brownie karim does gymnastics but sarah thinks shes no good at gym naveen isnt sporty at all one day sarah has a new idea and tells her mother she wants to try judo her mother thinking this an excellent idea rushes out to buy a leotard sarah knows you need a special suit for judo they take the leotard back and come home with a judo kit

Write out the following passage, adding the missing punctuation. Look out for all the capital letters.

we live in ealing part of london in the south east so we live in england but we also live in great britain the british isles and in the united kingdom its a bit complicated were also part of europe the british commonwealth which used to be the empire and we also live in the northern hemisphere sometimes its said that we live in the west but i dont understand this we might be west of europe but we are east of the united states so it doesnt mean anything it all depends on where you are

Write out the following passage, adding the missing punctuation.

naveen a thoughtful boy really likes computers he also likes dinosaurs and modern reptiles but his best friend a boy called karim is more interested in football and other sports he is always trying to get naveen who hates sport to go to a match with him but naveen who dislikes noisy crowds prefers to spend a saturday afternoon on his computer with his other friends luke simon sahib and vijay

Punctuating speech

This can be tricky as there are a lot of things to remember.

Speech marks

Speech marks enclose speech. Anything that is said must have speech marks before and after it. If a speech is interrupted by an 'asked Karim' or a 'complained Laura' you must remember to restart the speech marks.

For example:

- 'Why,' asked Karim, 'does it always rain on football days?'
- 'It's just not fair,' complained Laura, 'that everyone I know gets more pocket money than I do!'

Starting a new line

During a written **conversation**, if something is said by someone *other* than the last person who spoke, you must start a new line – indented (moved in to the right) slightly from the margin.

For example:

   'Hi, Karim!' called Naveen from the other side of the street. 'Where are you going? Somewhere interesting?'

   'Not really,' replied Karim.

   'Well, don't be so mysterious,' his friend urged. 'Is it a secret?'

   'Not at all,' said Karim. 'I'm going to buy a present for my sister.'

TOP TIP

Open any of your own story books on a page with conversation to see how this works.

Punctuation inside speech marks

As well as speech marks before and after anything that is said, all speech must have some punctuation when it ends.

- If what is said is at the end of the sentence, then it will end with a full stop, an exclamation mark or a question mark, for example:
  As he entered, he said, 'I'm going to buy a present for my sister.'

- If the sentence continues after what is said, then the speech can end with:

  - a comma, for example: 'Not really,' replied Karim.

  - an exclamation mark or question mark, for example: 'Hi, Karim!' called Naveen from the other side of the street.

Note that you cannot use a full stop at the end of the speech if the sentence continues.

TOP TIP

Remember that every speech, however short, must have some punctuation after it as well as the speech marks.

To do

Write out and put the missing punctuation into the following passages. You will need to think about starting new lines where appropriate and all the punctuation needed in conversations.

mr sloppys ice cream is declared sarah the best in the world rubbish replied naveen rudely my mums is loads better its made from real fruit so what said sarah mr sloppys couldnt be better lets see said naveen why dont we test them both on karim and laura and see whos right im right youll see retorted sarah nobodys better than mr sloppy and i should know because hes my dad

wheres my jacket yelled karims sister shireen from her room im late at the stables and its my turn to do the horses food theyll be starving its probably under your bed where i found your T-shirt socks sweatshirt and most of your underwear replied her overworked mum thanks mum shouted shireen but i cant find my jodhpurs thats the second pair this term sighed her mum despairingly i cant help it responded shireen jodhpurs arent cool anyway and mum dont get a shock when you come in but ive had my head shaved

Write out the following passage, adding capital letters, commas, full stops, apostrophes, question marks, exclamation marks, speech marks and punctuation inside the speech marks, and starting new lines where appropriate.

AIM HIGH

in the shops naveen met his friend karim. karim was with his mum who is a friend of naveens mum. the mums started talking at first naveen and karim did not mind then they got bored and karim who can be rather wild had an idea i am going to pile up all the cans of baked beans he said and i dare you to do it with the spaghetti hoops when the towers were higher than karim and naveen and about to topple over a shop assistant noticed what the boys had done the manager came over to the mums are these two boys with you he enquired watch out cried naveen the beans are falling over

TOP TIP
There are 46 things to add.

Write out the following passage, adding capital letters, commas, full stops, apostrophes, question marks, exclamation marks, speech marks and punctuation inside the speech marks, and starting new lines where appropriate.

look at my cat said laura shes got things crawling on her fur ugh screamed lauras mother whats the matter with her its disgusting what is it ive no idea mumbled lauras dad from behind his sons rice krispies packet who cares anyway sneered lauras brother paul a very tiresome boy cats stink its probably got fleas my friends sisters cat had fleas the size of gerbils

Here is an extract from a script. Turn it into a story, made up mostly of conversation, making sure you punctuate accurately and using good substitutes for 'said' or 'replied'. Be careful to make it clear who is speaking!

Lord Grandcastle: I can't sleep. Where's my minstrel? Fetch my minstrel!

Court Floormop: Immediately, your lordship. Minstrel! Call The Court Minstrel!

Minstrel: (enters panting) I'm here! I'm here! What's all the fuss?

Lord Grandcastle: I can't sleep. I've tried everything. Chocolate, hot baths, cold bath, jacuzzis and jumping… It's hopeless. Where've you been? I need you to entertain me.

Court Floormop (aside): For goodness sake, entertain him. Or none of us will get any sleep.

Minstrel: I'll have to go and get my lute. It's in the fridge.

Lord Grandcastle: Hurry! Hurry! This is desperate!

Court Floormop: Shall I fan your lordship, while we are waiting? Or would you like some more sweeties?

Lord Grandcastle: Sweeties? Yes. Of course, you idiot. Quick! It must be at least a minute since I ate the last packet. And fan me too. With your beard.

Minstrel: Here I am. Now, what do you want me to play?

Lord Grandcastle: Something noisy. I've got to get to sleep somehow.

Use one of the following ideas to practise writing a conversation. Make sure you create different characters through their individual ways of speaking and remember to punctuate the conversation accurately. NB This is a conversation, not a script, so you will need to use 'said' and 'replied' and more interesting substitutes for these words.

- Heard outside the staff room door.
- Left football boot to right football boot before or after the match.
- Before the party.
- After the party.
- Where shall we go on holiday?
- Persuasions:
  - Try to persuade your parents to let you go to a sleepover/party/bowling/ cinema/shopping centre.
  - Try to persuade your friend to come to a football match.
  - Try to persuade your parents to give you a mobile phone/puppy/TV for your birthday.
- Planning something.
- An argument.
- A confession.

Apostrophes

Apostrophes do two totally different jobs. They:
- show where one or more letters have been left out (**omission** or **contraction**)
- show that something belongs to someone or something (**possession**).

Omission

Where a word or words have been shortened – abbreviated – the apostrophe is put in to show where the letters have been taken out.

For example:	
I am	I'm
you are	you're
he is	he's
we had	we'd
they will	they'll

Possession

Some people think this is complicated but in fact there is one simple rule: the apostrophe goes after the last letter of whoever or whatever the thing belongs to.

For example:
Laura's foot
Sarah's house
Naveen's school
Karim's mum
The children's playground
The boys' ball.

Some people get confused by plurals but the rule does not change.

For example:

the room of the men	becomes	the men's room
the room of the ladies	becomes	the ladies' room

The last letter of 'men' is 'n' and the apostrophe goes after that.
The last letter of 'ladies' is 's' and the apostrophe goes after that.

Practise by turning these phrases around:

> For example: the hat of the lady = the lady's hat

the homework of Sarah
the gym of the school
the cages of the animals
the staff room of the teachers
the job of Mrs Watson
the car of Mr Das
the picnic of the families
the ideas of the professors
the speech of the president
the homes of the millionaire
the club of the men
the T-shirt of Thomas

Thomas

Write out the following passage, adding the missing apostrophes:

TOP TIP
There are 17 to add.

'Whats the point of going to Naveens house if Im not allowed to play in his tree house?' complained Karim. 'Naveens dads brilliant. Hes made this amazing tree house. Its got all kinds of gadgets and doors and clever things like windows that really open and a ladder that unfolds on its own. Were really boring in this family and theres nothing to do and dads no good at making things. Bens going to help his dad make a table. Theyve got brilliant tools in their shed. Anyway, the tree house is really safe and its the best tree house Ive ever seen and I will be fine with Naveens dad there, so, please Mum, say youll let me go!'

Three tips on apostrophes

1 Remember that you use apostrophes in two ways: if letters are missed out in an abbreviation or to show that something belongs to someone. Apostrophes are never needed in:

● ordinary verbs, such as 'wants', 'likes', 'runs'

● plurals, such as 'horses', 'puddings', 'trees', 'DVDs', except to show possession.

2 Don't confuse *it's* and *its*.

● *It's* = it is. The apostrophe is simply doing its first job: showing where a letter has been left out (in this case, the 'i' of 'is').

● *Its* = belonging to it. If something belongs to 'it', for example 'the giraffe bent *its* neck' – we do not add an apostrophe to show belonging. Think of it as being like 'his' – you wouldn't put an apostrophe in 'his'!

Copy and complete the following phrases by filling in the gaps with its or it's:

The dog wags _its_ tail
_It's_ my dog
My car has lost _its_ bumper
The spider made _its_ web
_It's_ a lovely day
My cat has lost _its_ collar
I think _it's_ going to rain
I'm afraid _it's_ broken!
Do you know _its_ name?

3 Don't confuse *you're* and *your*.

- *You're* = you are, for example 'you're a bit late', 'you're coming too', 'you're my best friend'.
- *Your* = belonging to you, for example 'your book ', 'your house', 'your friend'.

To do

Copy this conversation and fill in the blanks with the correct word or abbreviation: your/you're; its/it's

'Where's ~~your~~ rucksack? You've left ~~your~~ socks in it and they need washing.'

' ~~It's~~ in the car. I'll get it. ~~It's~~ a bit muddy. I dropped it on the pitch and it also broke ~~its~~ zip when I was running for the bus. Everything fell out. I might have lost ~~your~~ phone too. I think it just slipped out of ~~its~~ case.'

'I hope ~~your~~ ~~you're~~ having me on! ~~your~~ ✗ in big trouble if ~~you're~~ not! After you lost ~~your~~ phone you promised to be more careful!'

' ~~It's~~ not really my fault. I've been telling you about the zip for ages. The phone was useless anyway. ~~It's~~ lost ~~its~~ memory.'

'Well, ~~It's~~ not the only one, is it? ~~It's~~ a fine one to talk!'

Hyphens

Hyphens are used less now than they used to be but we still need them in:

- compound words
- pre-fixed words
- word breaks.

Compound words are words made up of two or more other words joined together with hyphens.

> For example: son-in-law, merry-go-round, forget-me-not, a build-up.

Pre-fixed words are words made up of a prefix joined to a word.

> For example: semi-detached, re-cover (to mean to put a new cover on something), pre-historic.

Word breaks use hyphens when there is not enough room to write or type a whole word on a line and it is necessary to break the word in two. It's usually best to begin the word on a new line, even if it means leaving a little more unused space than usual on the line above.

However, if it is a long word and it needs to be broken, try to break the word at a point when it breaks into its separate bits of meaning or when its sound – or **syllables** – break.

> For example:
> - clock-work rather than clockw-ork
> - break-fast rather than brea-kfast.

GRAMMAR

Grammar is the name we give to the **rules** and **guidelines** that help us express ourselves **clearly** and **accurately** and also help us work out what others want to tell us. Grammar matters because if something needs to be *said*, it also needs to be *understood*.

We use language in two main ways – we speak it and we write it. When we speak, we pay less attention to grammar than when we write.

For example:

- If you are telling your friend about something that happened to you, you will probably not think in sentences with full stops and new paragraphs.

- You will probably use lots of 'and's and colloquial (informal, chatty and relaxed) expressions.

- If you were to write the same story as an essay, you would pay more attention to structure, the sentences, paragraphs, more formal language, etc.

These days many people are pretty relaxed about grammar – even in written pieces – but it is worth learning the rules because they help you write clearly and accurately and because you sometimes need to write in a way that is appropriate for a particular purpose or a particular person.

This section on grammar is in two parts. Firstly, there is a brief description of **parts of speech**, for example verbs, nouns, etc. Then there are some reminders about **common grammatical mistakes** and **commonly confused words**.

Parts of speech

All words have a job to do – they name things, they describe them, they tell you what's being done, they join one idea to the next, they tell you where or when something happens.

Nouns

A **noun** is a **naming word**. All things – whether you can see, touch, smell, feel them or not – have names:

- common nouns, for example: cat, house, school, spoon, sausage
- proper nouns, for example: Laura, Birmingham, Africa, Prince William, Westminster Abbey
- abstract nouns, for example: kindness, light, warmth, fear, size
- collective nouns, for example: herd, group, swarm, flock, team.

If you can put 'a/an' or 'the' before a word and it makes sense, it will be a common, abstract or collective noun, for example: the dog, the smile, a pain, an assembly.

All words with capital letters are proper nouns and don't have 'a/an' or 'the' in front of them.

Adjectives

Words that **describe nouns** are called **adjectives**.

For example:
pretty, slow, heavy, noisy, hungry, difficult, clever, sleepy, quick, distant.

Verbs

Every sentence has some kind of **action** or **doing word** in it. These are called **verbs**. Verbs tell us whether something:

- is happening now (the present) or
- has already happened (the past) or
- will happen (the future).

These are called the tenses of the verb.

Present	Past	Future
sit	sat	will sit
think	thought	will think
walk	walked	will walk
eat	ate	will eat

Time flies like an arrow; fruit flies like a banana.

Think about it!

Flies can be a plural noun or a verb. How many other words can you think of that could be a noun or a verb? Write a sentence for each pair.

Adverbs

Sometimes we want words that **tell us more about verbs** – how, where or when the action of a verb happens. These words are called **adverbs**.

> For example:
> slowly, fast, madly, beautifully, well, late, heavily, often, away, cheerfully.

Adverbs add detail and feeling to a sentence, telling us more about the verb.

Here are some examples of sentences in which there are nouns and verbs and adverbs that tell you more about the verb:

- Naveen chews thoughtfully.
- The boy looked everywhere.
- Mrs Chinwicket woke early.

Write out the sentences below and underline the parts of speech as follows:

nouns like this ....   verbs like this - - - - - - -

adjectives like this / / / / / /   adverbs like this ~ ~ ~ ~

The banana was brought in on a lordly dish. My grandfather peeled it with a golden knife.

He then cut a sliver off and, with a golden fork, put it in his mouth and carefully tasted it.

Pronouns

We use **pronouns** in place of a noun. Pronouns include:

- he, she, I, you, we, they, them, us, me, him, her, his, it.

They help us to avoid repeating the noun.

> For example:
>
> - Oliver shouted to Oliver's brother and asked him to give Oliver Oliver's football.
>
> becomes
>
> - Oliver shouted to *his* brother and asked him to give *him his* football.

Prepositions

This is a big name for lots of little words that are used to give information about, usually, place or time. Here are some of the ones we use most often:

- in, under, between, through, at, for, with, to, after, off, on, over, beside, before, by, against, up, about, down, for, above, between.

To do Try writing a sentence of more than six or seven words without a preposition and you'll see how necessary they are.

TOP TIP
There are more than 100 prepositions in English. Find out some more.

Conjunctions or connectives

These are 'joining' words.

Conjunctions join two short sentences to make them one: and, but, because, although.

> For example, the following pairs of sentences flow more sensibly if we use a conjunction to join the two ideas:
>
> - It's raining. We still want to go out.   *becomes*
>   It's raining *but* we still want to go out.
>
> - I like riding bicycles. I like surfing big waves.   *becomes*
>   I like riding bicycles *and* I like surfing big waves.

Connectives are useful words that join an idea to a previous one.

> For example, the following pairs of ideas can be linked by using a connective. The second idea makes sense because it is connected to the first idea:
>
> - We don't want to go out. It's raining.   *becomes*
>   We don't want to go out *as* it's raining.
>
> - I am starving. I'm going to eat a whole large pizza by myself.   *becomes*
>   I am starving *so* I'm going to eat a whole large pizza by myself.

TOP TIP
Many connectives can also be conjunctions, for example, until, since, as, so.

To do Write ten sentences in which you have used at least one conjunction to connect two shorter sentences, for example:

I made a huge cooked breakfast. Everyone was so hungry.

could become

I made a huge cooked breakfast since everyone was so hungry.

Articles

We use 'the' and 'a' (or 'an') all the time.

- 'A'/'an' is called the **indefinite article**.
- 'The' is called the **definite article**.

Avoiding common mistakes

They're, there or their

Some people get these muddled as they sound the same. Here are some examples of how they are used correctly:

- Laura and Sarah will be late. *They're* (i.e. *they are*) staying at school for a rehearsal. *They're* my best friends.
- *There* (i.e. in a particular place) is my house. The one over *there*. *There* is no one in. I don't think *there* is any food either.
- I've put *their* (i.e. belonging to them) dinner in the fridge. They've gone to *their* friend's house. They like to do *their* homework together.

To do

Copy the passage below and fill in each gap with one of the following: *they're, there* or *their*.

Where are the boys? _____ looking for _____ football. It went somewhere over _____ in the bushes. _____ probably crawling about on _____ hands and knees getting _____ trousers muddy. It's nearly dark now so _____ isn't much point carrying on looking. _____ probably just enjoying getting dirty!

Wear, where, were or we're

These all sound similar and you need to be sure which one you want:

- What can I *wear* (i.e. clothing)? I need something new to *wear*.
- *Where* (i.e. in what place) is the remote control? It's not *where* I left it. Why can't people leave it *where* I put it?
- Why *were* (i.e. past tense of *are*) you so late? *Were* you at Naveen's house? We *were* worried about you.
- *We're* (i.e. *we are*) feeling sick. *We're* going to the bathroom. *We're* never going to eat three bags of popcorn again.

To do

Copy the passage below and fill in each gap with one of the following: *wear, where, were* or *we're*.

_____ going to have a party. _____ both going to be eleven and Sarah and I _____ discussing it all through lunch with our friends. The two problems are _____ to have it and what to _____. I'd like to have it in the hall _____ the disco was, as the lights _____ brilliant at Karim's party. _____ having a meeting to discuss it later. We _____ going to meet at Sarah's house as that is _____ I left the shoes I want to _____ but she can't find them. Do you know _____ your high-heeled shoes are so that I can paint them yellow?

Now make up ten sentences of your own, using these words appropriately.

TOP TIP

Your understanding of parts of speech may be tested in the 11+ exam in a simple and straightforward way so it's best to learn them all.

TOP TIP

They're over there with their friends.

Simple!

TOP TIP

'Where' always has a sense of place. One way to remember this is that it has the word 'here' inside it.

Practice or practise, etc

Practice or **practise**; **advice** or **advise**; **device** or **devise**; **licence** or **license**; **prophecy** or **prophesy**.

These five pairs of words have something interesting in common. The first one in each pair is a noun; the second one in each pair is a verb.

- You may have a piano *practice* (a thing, a noun) but you will *practise* (a doing word, a verb) the piano.

- I give you *advice* (noun) about your grammar and you *advise* (verb) me that you know all about it!

- You design a *device* (noun) to help you pump up your tyres and your brother *devises* (verb) a trick to get out of doing his homework.

- Your mother will have a driving *licence* (noun) but the manager of The Red Lion pub is *licensed* (verb) to sell alcohol.

- The weather man made a *prophecy* (noun) that it will be sunny tomorrow but he *prophesies* (verb) that the sun will shine.

To do / AIM HIGH

Copy this passage and try filling in the gaps with advice/advise, device/devise, practice/practise, licence/license, prophecy/prophesy. You may need to change some of the tenses.

After football _practice_ _____ at school, Naveen rushes home to _practise_ _____ his ball skills. Ali, his father, has _____ a programme to help him and tries to _advise_ him but Naveen doesn't want his dad's _advise_. He prefers to watch his Premiership video and get all the _advice_ he wants from that. 'I get loads of _advice_ at school,' he tells his dad, 'and loads of _advice_ from my teacher, too!'

'Ah!' said Ali. 'But I _____ that you will do much better if you _____ my programme. I have _____ it specially for you! And I've just got my coaching _licence_ _____!'

Effect or affect

This is also about the difference between a noun and a verb.

- Traffic fumes have a bad *effect* on Rajiv's asthma. They *affect* him adversely.

Effect is a noun and *affect* is a verb.

To do / AIM HIGH

Copy the following passage and fill in the gaps:

'I don't think that late nights have a good _____ on your concentration,' said Sarah's mother after Sarah had fallen asleep over her homework.

'It's not the late nights that _____ me,' replied Sarah. 'It's the _____ of having to get up early in the mornings!'

'An understandable _____,' remarked her father, 'for someone who reads in bed until 3.00am! How can you not expect so little sleep to _____ how you feel the next day?'

'Oh Sarah!' sighed her mother. 'What _____ will that have on your gym display today?'

Choose or chose; lose or loose

These words are often confused. You need to think about how they sound. Here are the correct uses:

- I *choose* my friends.
- I *lose* my watch.

The two above sound the same.

- I *chose* my present (i.e. I did this yesterday).
- My window is *loose*.

TOP TIP

These just need to be learnt and practised.

Copy the following passage and fill in the gaps:

Will you help me _____ a new hair slide? The clasp on my old one has become _____ and I need to get a new one as I'm bound to _____ this one before long! It keeps falling off. My gran _____ one for me last week but it was pink, and I hate pink. I can't believe she _____ it. I might even *try* to _____ it.

To or too

These words sound the same and look very similar, so they are often confused.

'Too' always has a sense of 'as well' or 'more than you need':

- Karim went and Naveen went *too*.
- Karim ate *too* much pizza and Naveen was *too* full to finish his.

In all other instances (except, of course, when you mean the number two) use 'to':

- I go *to* school.
- I am trying *to* finish this sum.
- Can you tell me how *to* get *to* the station?

Copy the following passage and fill in the blanks with either 'too' or 'to':

'We're going _____ have a picnic. Do you want _____ come _____?'

'Not much. What's there _____ do on a picnic? Anyway, I'm _____ tired and it's _____ wet. It's probably going _____ rain again, _____!'

'What a misery you are! Aren't you going _____ do anything today? Do come! I'm going _____ make a lovely picnic. Sarah and Laura are coming _____ and we may go _____ the pond _____ hire a boat.'

'Oh all right! But I won't do anything _____ energetic. And I want _____ eat a lot _____. Understand?'

'_____ right! You always do!'

Properly or probably

These two useful words can sound similar but they have completely different meanings.

- Laura's little brother can't tie his shoelaces *properly*.
- Do speak *properly*! I can't understand you when you mumble!
- I want to play the piano *properly*.

- We're *probably* going to Spain for our holiday.
- It will *probably* stop raining soon.
- If you really tried you could, very *probably*, pass this exam.

You will find an exercise to help you practise these below.

Uninterested or disinterested

These two words do *not* mean the same thing.

*Un*interested means having no interest in a subject, that it is boring.

> For example:
>
> - The class was *uninterested* in the talk about moths and they fidgeted all through it.
> - I tried to get my dog to eat the cold spaghetti but he was *uninterested* and ate my ice cream instead!

*Dis*interested means having nothing personal to gain from something.

> For example:
>
> - It is hard to find a *disinterested* referee as most of the parents have a child in the competition.
> - The company sent the scientist's new invention to a *disinterested* expert for an assessment before they decided whether or not to buy it (i.e. the expert had nothing to gain from the invention so his opinion would be completely honest and unbiased).

TO do — AIM HIGH

Copy this passage and put the correct word in the gap: properly/probably; uninterested/disinterested

'We'll _____ go to the museum tomorrow,' Rajiv's mum told him. 'I really want you to look _____ at those dinosaurs so you can get down to your project.'

'I can do the project from the internet,' argued Rajiv. 'I am completely __✗__ in dinosaurs and I'd rather play with Karim.'

'Well, Karim's mum said she and Karim would come too,' replied his mum, 'which is kind and totally _____ on their part as Karim's project is on engines.'

'Now I'm __✗__ confused,' complained Rajiv. 'Karim said he would _____ be at his dad's office tomorrow.'

'He _____ changed his mind,' said Rajiv's mum.

Except or accept

These two words sound alike but the meanings are completely different. See how they are used in the following sentences:

● Everyone played cricket *except* Karim and Naveen.

● *Except* for geography, I like everything I do at school.

● Laura cannot *accept* Sarah's invitation as she will be staying with her grandmother.

● Rajiv said he was sorry for crashing the car but his parents would not *accept* his apology.

Copy the following passage and fill in the gaps using one or other of the above words:

Everyone _____ Naveen came to Karim's party. His mother had telephoned to _____ the invitation but he didn't turn up. Karim refused to start the game without him. 'No-one _____ Naveen understands how to play,' he complained.

'I can't _____ that,' said Tom. 'I can read the instructions and teach everyone else.'

'That would be fine,' said Karim, '_____ that you're holding them upside down.'

'Let's have tea,' suggested his mum. 'Naveen did _____ your invitation so I'm sure he's on his way.'

'OK,' said Karim, 'we can eat everything _____ the salt and vinegar crisps because they're Naveen's favourite.'

Fewer or less

These two words mean different things so it is worth learning which is which.

● *Fewer* is used when you are talking about *a number* of individual objects, for example people, shops, presents, biscuits, etc.

● *Less* is used for *an amount* of something, for example meat, noise, water, money.

TOP TIP

A good way to remember is to think of *fewer* sugar lumps but *less* sugar. Another might be *fewer* bottles but *less* water.

Copy the passage and try putting the appropriate word in the blanks:

Laura decided to invite her four best friends to dinner rather than have a birthday party this year. Her mother was pleased. '_____ friends means _____ mess,' she said.

'_____ friends means _____ presents too,' replied Laura, ruefully.

'_____ spilled drink, _____ sausages trodden into the carpet, _____ crisp crumbs under the table, _____ waste paper and _____ tears when people don't win all the games. Sounds good to me,' mused Laura's mother.

'And _____ fun too,' thought Laura, beginning to change her mind.

Compliment or complement

A **compliment** is something you say that makes people feel good about themselves. The following are all *compliments*:

You do look nice! I love your T-shirt! Wow, that's clever!

Compliment can be a verb or a noun:

- He *complimented* (verb) me on my exam results.

- I had loads of *compliments* (noun) on my new haircut.

A **complement** is something that gives a feeling of completeness to something else:

- Mango chutney is the perfect *complement* to a chicken biriyani.
- My blue scarf *complements* my red jacket – it really sets it off.
- Our new goalie is a good *complement* to the squad which only had a part-timer before.

Complement can be a verb or a noun:

- The conservatory *complements* (verb) our sitting room beautifully.
- The mustard was a good *complement* (noun) to the gammon steak.

TOP TIP

These may be the two most confused words in English.

Copy the passage below and fill in each gap with one of the following: compliment or complement. You may need to change the tense of one or two words.

Judge Grumpus met Mrs Chinwicket at the station. 'May I say,' he whispered in her ear, 'how utterly charming you look today?' She beamed at this unexpected _____i_____. 'And,' he continued, dribbling slightly, 'that your green scarf is the perfect _____e_____ to your extraordinary complexion. A quite remarkable colour match!' Mrs Chinwicket felt she should _____i_____ Judge Grumpus in return, only it was hard to know what to say. The colour of his brown tie was not _____e_____ by the custard stains down his front and the cat hairs around his bristly chin made it hard to _____i_____ his appearance in general.

Should've; could've; would've; might've

On page 15 we looked at how to use the apostrophe in abbreviations. The concern with these words, however, is not so much one of punctuation, as the way the words sound. Some people think the 've' sounds like 'of' and then write it that way.

TOP TIP

Make sure you understand the difference and *never* write 'should of'.

Look at the following examples:

- '*Have* you done your homework?'
  'No, but I *should have*. I *should have* done my homework.'

- 'Where's Naveen? He *should have* been here ages ago.'
  '*Has* he telephoned?'
  'No, but he *should have*.'

When you read these examples, you can hear that *have* is the right word to use – for the sentences to make sense. This is exactly the same for *could have* and *would have* and *might have*. There is no problem abbreviating it to *should've* but you should never use 'of' in this context.

Copy the passage below and fill in the blanks using should have, could have, would have or might have. Then write it out again, substituting the abbreviated versions (should've, etc).

'I can't find my homework book,' said Karim.

'Did you leave it at school?' asked his mum, while she was putting the shopping away.

'I _____,' admitted Karim, 'but it _____ been on the top of my desk and I _____ seen it when I was packing my bag.'

'Well, you _____ been more careful,' said Karim's mum. 'I _____ thought you _____ learned to remember important things by now.'

'I suppose I _____ dropped it somewhere,' Karim wondered. 'Oh well, I'll have my burger now and I'll ring Naveen about the homework afterwards.'

'Burgers!' exclaimed his mother. 'I knew I'd forgotten something!'

'Hm,' muttered Karim. 'I _____ thought you _____ learned to remember important things by now.'

Me or I

The rule for when to use *me* and when to use *I* is very straightforward. If you want to write a sentence in which two or more people are involved instead of one, you still use *me* when you normally would and *I* when you normally would.

For example:

- The head teacher gave the prize to *me*. (Not … gave the prize to *I*.)
- The head teacher gave the prize to John and *me*. (Not … gave the prize to John and *I*.)

Just because you have added John does not mean that *me* changes to *I*.

Similarly:

- *I* went out. (Not *Me* went out.)
- John and *I* went out. (Not John and *me* went out or *Me* and John went out.)

Just because John comes too, does not mean that *I* changes to *me*.

Copy the following passage and fill in the blanks with either I or me. Remember that whether or not you are the only person in the sentence makes no difference to whether you should use I or me.

Rajiv gave presents to Karim and _me_. Laura gave sweets to Sarah and _me_. I gave the books to Karim, and Laura and _I_ gave the game to Rajiv. When Karim and _I_ opened our presents, I was surprised as Rajiv had given Laura and _I_ exactly what we had given him!

Copy the passage below and fill in each space, using one of the following: Laura and me, Laura and I, me and Laura, I and Laura.

Mrs Chinwicket called ____Laura me____ to her desk and she was clearly cross with us. ____Laura I____ had just been sitting in the playground and couldn't think of any reason that we might be in trouble. Mrs Chinwicket looked sternly at ____Laura me____ and snarled. 'What have you to say for yourselves?' she demanded. I tried to speak but my voice sounded very small.

'What have ____Laura I____ done?' I asked.

e.g. or i.e.

These abbreviations get used all the time and are very useful but they mean completely different things.

e.g. is an abbreviation of *exempli gratia* which means *for example*:

● My vet specialises in small animals, e.g. tortoises, birds, guinea pigs and hamsters.

i.e. stands for *id est* which means *that is*:

● I've got to get my application in really soon i.e. by Tuesday which is the closing date.

Copy the following passage and fill in the blanks, using the correct abbreviation:

I'm having a party really soon _i.e._ on Saturday and I've got loads to get ready, _e.g._ the food, the drinks, clearing the room and something to wear. My best friend, _i.e._ Sarah, is coming to help and she's bringing quite a lot of stuff, _e.g._ balloons, decorations, some of the food and so on. I'm a bit worried about one thing _i.e._ the weather, as I really want to be outside but there's nothing I can do about that. With luck, the main event, _i.e._ the fireworks, will be fine.

Opposites

It would be straightforward if all opposites began with 'un' or 'dis'. Sadly, they don't! Simple words do take 'un' or 'dis' as their opposites:

TOP TIP

Don't assume that you can make an opposite with 'un' or 'dis'. Check in your dictionary!

For example:	
pleasure	displeasure
like	dislike
do	undo
kind	unkind

However, we often put 'in' at the start of the word to make an opposite and 'in' changes to 'im' or 'il' or 'ir' if the rest of the word sounds better that way:

For example:	
correct	incorrect
sane	insane
proper	improper
polite	impolite
legal	illegal
liberal	illiberal
regular	irregular

2 IMPROVING YOUR WRITING SKILLS

This chapter focuses on improving your writing skills by looking at the different styles of writing that are appropriate to different tasks, giving you lots of tips and methods for making your writing both clear and interesting and focusing on the importance of developing your vocabulary.

WRITING APPROPRIATELY

We ask a lot from **language**. We expect it to do a huge number of jobs. We use it to:

- explain
- persuade
- discuss
- describe
- teach
- tell stories.

TOP TIP
Language has to be very flexible and always ready to change jobs.

We put it into any number of different forms, for example:

- letters
- diaries
- interviews
- TV and radio scripts
- speeches
- novels
- advertisements
- instructions
- poems
- non-fiction
- plays
- lists

and you can probably think of more.

It's as though it has to keep changing its clothes in order to perform differently for us. Sometimes we need it to be **serious** and **formal** – as though it's wearing a suit; sometimes it can be **relaxed** and **lively** – as if it's in beach clothes! At other times we want it to be just **useful** and **plain** – as if it's in jeans and a T-shirt.

We write in different ways according to the job we want the language to do. Sometimes we:

- have to write simply and clearly, e.g. when giving instructions or directions

- want to write enthusiastically and amusingly, e.g. when sending a postcard home

- want to sound serious and responsible, e.g. when apologising

- want our language to be brisk and eye-catching, e.g. if we are advertising something.

By looking at these different styles of writing and trying them out for yourself, you will be improving your writing skills and preparing yourself for the exam.

AIM HIGH

Speeches

Speeches have to capture and hold people's attention. They can also be entertaining and full of little stories, anecdotes or memories – think of the speeches at weddings. Other speeches try to persuade someone of a point of view and get them to change their mind. The important thing is not to waste words but to make what you have to say clear and interesting.

On the following page is an example of how you might start:

TOP TIP
A speech needs to grab the audience's attention from the start.

▶

To do

AIM HIGH

Write a speech that you could make:

- at a party to celebrate your best friend's winning a gold medal in an important competition
- in a school discussion about whether your school should or should not have uniform.

Interviews

Interviews are a way of **getting information**. This information might be about the lives and opinions of famous or important people or essential facts that a policeman or a doctor or a lawyer needs to know.

Good interviews use 'open' rather than 'closed' questions. **Open questions** invite the interviewee to answer fully and interestingly.

Examples of open questions include:

- Can you explain how it felt when …?
- Would you tell me about your …?
- What happened when you went to …?

Closed questions tend to be answered with a simple 'yes' or 'no' and don't help the interview along.

Examples of closed questions include:

- Do you usually wear trainers?
- Do you live in Cambridge?
- Have you been to America?

Open questions usually enable the interviewer to pick up on what the interviewee has said and move on to something interesting that has come up in the answer.
Closed questions tend to result in a boring list of short answers.

Write one of the following:

- An interview between you and someone you like or admire. If you can, do a real interview. This will involve writing down the questions beforehand and then noting down the answers. Alternatively, make up the whole interview – both the questions and the answers.

- Imagine you are a policeman interviewing someone who has been caught with stolen property. Write the conversation. Remember you are trying to find out the truth.

- You have just been picked for your local professional football club's junior side. The local paper's reporter comes to interview you. Write the interview that appears in the paper at the end of the week.

TOP TIP

Try interviewing a grandparent or other adult and ask them about their childhood.

Newspaper reports

A **newspaper report** should be **clear** and **factual** and **answer the questions**: What? When? Where? Who? How? Why?

Some newspapers also try to **influence** the way readers respond to a story by their choice of language.

> Look, for example, at these two headlines:
>
> - Bug-ridden Burger Bar Forced to Close over Health Alarm!
> - Popular local take-away closes temporarily over hygiene concerns
>
> The first example makes the closure of the bar seem very dramatic by using an exclamation mark, by using the worrying words 'bug-ridden' and 'health alarm' and by using alliteration of the letter 'b' to make it sound very strong and punchy (see page 49). The second example expresses an opinion by describing the take-away as 'popular' but is less obviously intended to alarm the readers.

As already mentioned, a good newspaper report, like the one below, will provide answers to the questions:

What? When? Where? Who? How? Why?

Tabby in Dramatic Gerbil Rescue

Screams broke through the calm of a quiet Whiskerton side street last Sunday afternoon. Petra Noff watched her gerbil, Usain, scoot out of his cage. 'He bolted,' she told our reporter. 'He'd never done it before but there was a loud bang on the TV and he just shot off when I was cleaning his cage.'

Her neighbour, Lionel Plate, heard the commotion and sent his tabby cat, Sergeant, to the rescue. 'He's very gentle,' said Lionel. 'You wouldn't think so to look at him but he wouldn't hurt a fly.'

Sure enough, Sergeant followed Usain up the tree outside the flats and brought him carefully down between his teeth. 'I used to keep rats,' Lionel explained, 'and Sergeant always had to bring them down from the top of the cupboard. He never ate them – or not often.'

Needless to say, Petra was very relieved and Sergeant had a sardine supper as a reward last Sunday. 'The odd thing is,' explained Petra, 'that Usain had never climbed anything before. Now I'm always finding him hanging from the lampshade. I'm thinking of taking him skiing.'

Write a report for your local paper on:

- the opening of a new sports centre by a famous sports personality
- a traffic accident involving a car driving on the wrong side of the road
- a local child winning a national competition – this could involve a brief interview
- the proposed demolition of a local school to be replaced by a newly built one.

TOP TIP

Remember that, as a reporter, you should write factually. If you want to influence the way your information is received, however, you can experiment with emotive language.

Diaries

Diaries are usually **private** and written only for the writer to read. Therefore the writing can be as **informal**, as **casual** and as **honest** as you like. Exceptions include political and historical diarists who write with the intention of being read by others and therefore sometimes use more formal language.

To do

Write:

- the diary entries for a newly qualified teacher the day before and the day after she starts her first job
- a week in the diary of a ghost
- a week in the diary of a dog.

Advertisements

Advertisements are attempts to **persuade** people to buy. They need to be **eye-catching** and the number of words used is **limited**, so those words need to be **forceful** and **effective**.

To do

Write an advertisement for:

- a holiday resort that caters especially for families
- a new dog or cat food
- a car that runs on a new environmentally friendly fuel
- a newly launched fizzy drink.

When you have finished, see if you can cut out any unnecessary words.

TOP TIP

Look at the advertisements in a magazine or newspaper and see how few words are used compared to the space the picture takes.

Scripts

Plays, TV and radio programmes and TV ads all need **scripts**. It is important that the **individuals** in the script each have a **characteristic way of speaking**.

> For example, an aged man in pain with his joints would speak in a different way from a busy shopkeeper with lots of customers to serve.

Read this example of a script and notice how the two characters have different ways of speaking:

Mrs Bunn: Don't you worry, pet. Here's a nice cuppa tea and help yourself to a slice of cake – it's just out of the oven.

Mr Bunn: You're spoiling that child! It's about time he took some responsibility! When I was a lad, I'd never have got away with behaviour like that. My father would've walloped me – good and proper! *(thumps his cushion)*

Mrs Bunn:	There now, don't get into such a flap. Have some cake and leave the lad alone. Put your slippers on – they're warming by the fire – and let's play a nice game of Scrabble.
Mr Bunn:	Slippers! I never had slippers when I was a lad. One pair of boots was good enough for me!

Try to get a sense of character into these brief scripts:

- two dogs meet in the park
- Queen Molly and her maid Gwen prepare for a palace ball
- the team manager gives a pep talk to the team before a big match or competition
- three children get lost on a school trip.

Instructions and directions

Like advertisements, **instructions** and **directions** need to be **clear** and **uncomplicated** so that they can be understood.

> For example, read these clear, straightforward instructions:
>
> **HOW TO POLISH YOUR SHOES**
> Open your tin of shoe polish, making sure it's the right colour for your shoes. With a clean cloth, take out a little polish and spread it on the right shoe. Continue until the whole shoe is covered with a very thin layer of polish. Now do the same with the left shoe. Let the polish sink into the shoe for a few minutes. Take a shoe brush and brush the right shoe with quick rhythmic strokes until the polish is worked in and a deep shine appears. Make sure you do this with the whole shoe and then repeat with the left shoe. You may like to finish the process by rubbing the shoes gently with a clean soft cloth.

Write instructions for:

- sending an email
- cooking a light meal, e.g. an omelette or cheese on toast
- pumping up a bicycle tyre
- cleaning out a guinea pig's cage
- planting a bulb.

When you have finished, read your instructions through and check that they tell you exactly what to do.

TOP TIP
Instructions must be clear, concise and accurate.

Write directions for getting from the kitchen to your bedroom, noting various landmarks such as bookcases, radiators, stairs, doors, etc on the way.

Try one or more of the following:

- You have a friend who wants to learn how to swim. Explain, as carefully – and as encouragingly – as you can, how it is done, remembering to give any warnings you feel necessary.
- Explain how to play any game or sport you know well. You will need to describe clearly both the rules and techniques.
- Give clear instructions to a friend who wants to do one of the following: cook a simple meal, groom an animal.
- Give clear directions to a friend who needs to get from their house to your school.

You could also make up an imaginary recipe – or spell – for:
- getting homework done quickly
- making a horrible neighbour invisible
- turning my football boots into goal scorers.

You will need to use your imagination for these but should still make sure that they are detailed and move logically from one step to the next.

For example, here is a spell Sarah wrote to stop her Auntie Harriet coming to stay. It was very effective:

Ingredients: Disgusting hair slides Auntie Harriet sent for my birthday,
2 squirts of bathroom cleaner,
1 cup of vinegar,
2 cups of dust from the bottom of the vacuum cleaner bag,
paper with Auntie Harriet's name on it.

Instructions: Take all ingredients outside plus a bowl and wooden spoon.
Break hair slides into bowl.
Squirt with bathroom cleaner and pour over vinegar.
Add dust.
Tear up paper into four strips. Drop into bowl.

Mix well, while saying:
Magic spell. Do this well.
Keep Aunt Harriet away.
Do not let her come today.
Nor on any other day.
Magic spell hear what I say!

Dig hole in garden and bury mixture. Cover carefully. Jump on it ten times.

WRITING CLEARLY

It is **essential** that your writing is **clear** – that your reader can understand what it is you are trying to say. Clear is **simple** and **precise** and you should use it for comprehension answers, essays and, in fact, your written work in all subjects. The following exercises will help you to **improve the clarity of your writing**.

AIM HIGH

Meet the Blob

One way of practising clear writing is to try communicating with the Blob from Mars. The Blob is an intelligent creature who can be your pen-friend or, perhaps, someone you chat to by email or on the internet. The Blob knows and understands a lot about our world and how we live but, now and then, writes back to say that there was a word in your last message he didn't know, such as 'door' or 'bucket'. The Blob understands words such as 'horizontal', 'round', 'upright' and so on, so you can use them in your explanations.

To do

Explain the following to the Blob:

a needle	a shoe
a mug	a comb
a plate	a pencil
a watering can	a belt
a button	a flower-pot
a coin	a ruler
an escalator	a fire engine
a fork	a lemon
a knife	a candle
a table	a bed

a chair

a hairbrush

a bottle

TOP TIP

It helps to think about what the object looks like, and how that relates to what it is for.

TOP TIP

Get an adult or friend to have a go at this too. It is surprisingly tricky to explain ordinary, everyday objects.

To do

AIM HIGH

Once you have got the idea, you can try to explain more complicated ideas, such as:

- tiredness
- darkness
- hunger
- friendship
- fear
- home – this means more than just the place where you live
- making a decision
- having fun

TOP TIP

You can also play this as a game. Describe an object – as if to the Blob – and see if the other person can guess what it is.

Write for younger children

Do you sometimes look over what you have written and wonder what you meant to say?

Writing for younger children is **useful practice** for people who can get **tangled up** in their writing. You have to concentrate on making your meaning **straightforward** and expressing yourself in **clear** and **simple language**.

Whether you are writing stories, explanations, descriptions or instructions, you can still write about important things and write in detail but it is best to:

- write in short sentences
- use only words you are sure a younger child will know or could guess easily
- leave out any unnecessary information
- move a story along quickly
- put in enough detail so that your meaning or the important points in a story are clear.

To do

Try one of the following, remembering to write simply and clearly:

- Retell the story of any fairy tale, fable or legend you know.
- Look back at 'Tabby in Dramatic Gerbil Rescue' on page 31. Tell the story from Usain's point of view.
- Write an article for a children's magazine on one of the following:
  - how to look after a pet
  - how to maintain a bicycle
  - what to pack when you go on holiday
  - what you think makes good parents.

Think about sentences

Long sentences are usually unnecessary and it is easy to get muddled. Remember that a sentence should contain one main idea. A new idea deserves a sentence of its own. Short sentences help to make your writing clear. **A mix of long and short sentences** is much more interesting to read, keeps your reader involved and is also more fun to write.

TOP TIP

Remember, a sentence need be only two words, e.g. Sarah jumped.

To do

Here is a short piece composed of two very long sentences. Rewrite it in short sentences to make it clearer and more readable. You can take out and add words and punctuation, if it helps.

Claude the Crocodile was waiting for his lunch which he knew would be likely to come downstream if he waited long enough which was quite tricky as his tummy was rumbling and he'd had nothing since the men in the small boat whom he'd crunched up early that morning before the sun was properly up and with whom he would probably not have bothered if he'd had any idea how bony they would be. Claude yawned, his teeth glimmered in the afternoon light and his long pink tongue flopped over the side of his shining jaw but was he seeing correctly; could that be a small human coming along, looking absolutely yummy?

WRITING INTERESTINGLY

Focus on the vocabulary

English has developed by taking in words from other cultures and languages.

One result of this rich mix is that English has more **synonyms** – words that have the same meanings as other words – than any other language. This means that we have **many words to choose from** and it means we can write in many **different styles**. Having so many words at our disposal means we can write very **exciting** and **varied** English – we can work out our own style of writing and be quite adventurous.

Your choice of words will determine whether what you write is interesting or not.

For example, look at the two passages below and see how much livelier they would be if the words in brackets were used:

'You're not going to watch that gardening programme?' said (gasped) Karim.
'Yes, I am,' said (retorted) Mum.
'But I've got to watch the football on the other side,' said (exclaimed) Karim.
'I'm afraid not,' said (disagreed) Mum. 'You know I always watch this programme.'
'But it's the final!' said (protested) Karim. 'I've waited all season for this and one gardening programme is just like any other.'
'Not to me it isn't,' said (smiled) Mum. 'You'll have to go round to Naveen's.'

Sarah went (crept) out of the classroom. She went (slunk) out of school, sucking her lolly. She went (dawdled) along the road and went (slouched) past the shops, the cinema and her brother's nursery. As she went (trudged) down her own street, she went (plodded) even more slowly. How could she give her mother the letter from her teacher?

To make your writing more **interesting** to read, you should focus on the **individual words** that you use. Don't settle for the obvious but choose words with more colour, adding life and flavour to your writing. Think in terms of:

- the mood, age and appearance of your characters
- the setting of your story
- the time of day
- the weather

and so on.

You can often replace a verb and an adverb with a single verb, e.g. 'dawdled' or 'ambled' instead of 'went slowly'.

Look at the alternatives to 'said' used below depending on who the character is and the circumstances he is in. Perhaps George:

- is a farmer with crops dying for lack of rain: 'It's raining!' George *cheered*.
- is seven today and he has planned an outdoor birthday party: 'It's raining,' George *sniffed*.
- has waited all day to go out: 'It's raining,' George *grumbled*.
- is in the Sahara Desert: 'It's raining!' George *gasped*.
- has just finished painting the shed: 'It's raining!' George *fumed*.

To do

Think of as many substitutes for the word 'said' as you can. You could start by thinking of all the words that come from our expression of animal noises, e.g. growled, hissed, chirped, purred, bellowed, cackled, barked.

See pages 80–81 for some suggestions.

TOP TIP
There are at least 200 alternatives to the word 'said' so always try to think of one to use instead.

To do

Think of as many substitutes as you can for the word 'went' in the following sentence:

- Helen went up the road.

Here are a few suggestions: dawdled, ambled, raced, stumbled, tottered, skipped, bounced, galloped, limped, charged, skidded, waded, crawled, slithered, stalked.

See pages 81–82 for some more suggestions.

To do

Copy the following extract and find lively words to put in the blanks:

Laura _____ into the dark room. 'Is anyone here?' she _____ . There was silence except for a faint rustling. 'Hello?' she _____ again. 'Is there…?' Behind her, she heard the creaking of a floorboard and quickly she turned and _____ back towards the door. It shut suddenly in front of her. 'Help!' she _____ but her voice was almost a whisper. She _____ towards a sliver of light at the other end of the room. It flickered slightly as she _____ closer. She swallowed. 'Sarah!' she _____ . 'Sarah! 'Where are you?'

   'Sarah isn't here,' _____ a low voice. 'Sarah is a long way from here….'

3 THE EXAM

This chapter focuses on the exam: by giving advice on comprehension; information on how to approach each of the different types of essay that you may write in the exam; practice exercises so you have plenty of experience of writing in these different styles; and, finally, a section of exam-style practice exercises for comprehension and essay writing.

COMPREHENSIONS

Comprehension means understanding. A comprehension exercise is one that **tests your ability to read and understand** – both the **passage** set and the **questions** that follow it. You need to read the passage and the questions **carefully** and **read between the lines**. This means looking for things that the writer wants you to know but leaves you to work out for yourself.

Some very keen readers do surprisingly poorly on comprehensions, simply because they are used to reading quickly. If you are a quick reader, you must slow down and read slowly and carefully to take in the necessary detail.

The passage

- Read the passage carefully before you read the questions.

- Then look through the questions to get an idea of what they are asking.

- Then read the passage again – just as carefully.

Once you have understood the passage, you should not need to trawl through it again and again for the answer to each new question – though a quick check is reassuring.

There may be words in the passage that you don't know but don't worry – other pupils may not know them either. You can probably work out their meaning by the **context** (how the words are used in the passage).

> For example, in the sentence, 'It was clear from the *alacrity* with which Patterson entered the room that someone was after him', 'alacrity' could only mean a few things. (It means speed.)

Occasionally, the passage is *not* a passage but a **poem**. Again, you need to read the poem carefully but bear in mind that it is a poem and that means the writer has chosen to say what he or she wanted to say in that form for a reason. You therefore need to pay attention to **rhyme**, **rhythm**, **metaphors**, etc in addition to everything else. See page 58 for a comprehension based on a poem. There is another one on page 62 to try.

TOP TIP
Read the passage slowly and carefully – pretend you are a detective searching out the clues hidden in the passage in order to solve the questions.

TOP TIP
Time spent on grasping the passage is time saved on decoding the questions.

TOP TIP
Don't spend too long on individual words that you don't know. It is more important that you get a sense of the story or meaning of the whole passage.

TOP TIP
It is important to read instructions at the top of the paper as this often gives information on the passage. Missing it out can make understanding the passage harder.

The questions

Comprehension questions can:

- be purely factual, e.g. 'What was the burglar's name?'
- ask you to select material, e.g. 'Which of the animals named in the passage are mammals?'
- ask you to summarise, e.g. 'What were Emil's reasons for leaving the train?'
- ask you to make deductions, e.g. 'Why do you think the servant felt impatient?'
- ask you to develop ideas or themes contained in the passage or give your own response, e.g. 'What do you think happens next?' or 'What do you like about the passage?'
- be in two parts, in which case you need to be careful to answer the whole question – not just the first bit, e.g. 'How many people enter the room? How do you know?'

You will not be required to use knowledge or information from anywhere other than the passage, though common sense is often useful.

Most papers tell you the **number of marks** each question is **worth**. This is a valuable tool, so be sure to use it. Don't spend ages on a question that is only worth two marks and, therefore, leave no time for the last question which may be worth eight marks.

TOP TIP

If you find you are giving answers based on your own knowledge, rather than on information in the passage, you have probably misunderstood the question. A passage will contain all the information needed to answer the questions.

TOP TIP

Look ahead and make sure you leave enough time for the most valuable questions, i.e. the ones that are worth a lot of marks.

The answers

Full sentences or one-word answers

The instructions at the top of the paper should make it clear whether you need to write your answers as full sentences. Many papers require full sentence answers for some questions and only a one-word answer for others.

Remember a sentence:

- makes sense on its own
- has a noun (a subject) and a verb.

So, if you are asked to answer the question 'Why do you think Patterson hides under the bed?' with a complete sentence:

- do not write 'because he is scared'
- write 'Patterson hides because he is scared'.

You do not, however, need to write out the whole question in your answer.

TOP TIP

Do not begin with 'because' when asked for a complete sentence as you must answer the question fully and as instructed.

For example, in answer to the question 'When Patterson hears the footsteps coming down the long corridor, what does he do?':

- do not write: 'When Patterson hears the footsteps coming down the long corridor, he jumps out of the window.'
- write: 'When he hears the footsteps, he jumps out of the window.'

If the question only requires a one-word answer, don't waste time writing out a full sentence. In answer to the question 'What is the man's name?':

- do not write 'His name is Patterson'
- write 'Patterson'.

Leave spaces

Leave a **couple of lines** after each **answer**. In the checking time at the end you may realise that you have answered only half the question or that there is quite a lot more you could say to strengthen your answer. It is much better if you can fit this in straight after what you have already written rather than cramming it in over the top or using an asterisk to indicate that the rest of the answer is elsewhere on the paper.

Timing

It is obviously important to finish the paper on time, but you will not get any extra marks for finishing first.

If you finish early, don't sit back and watch everyone else write but use every spare minute you have to check what you have written and how you have written it.

TOP TIP

The paper is designed to enable good/average candidates to finish in time – just.

Checking

Try to leave some time at the end of comprehension tests for **checking**. You will know whether you often misspell and miss out words and therefore need lots of time to do this or whether you usually write accurately and clearly and can therefore do your checking in just a few minutes.

Checking can show up all kinds of errors that you may have missed when writing your answers and can, therefore, rescue vital marks. Ideally, you will have time to read through your answers, carefully, twice.

On the **first read-through** ask yourself the following about each question:

- Does my answer make sense? Does it explain clearly and accurately what I wanted to say?
- Does it answer the question I was asked?
- Does it answer the *whole* question I was asked?
- Is it the same answer as I gave to another question? (If it is, look at the questions again, as no two answers should be the same.)
- Have I written enough? (If a question is worth 8 marks, it will require a fuller answer than a question worth 2 marks.)

Then check to see if you have left any gaps. If you have, add some kind of answer. A blank space cannot earn you any marks. Even a wild guess may be partially right and earn a mark or two.

On the **second read-through** ask yourself the following about each question:

- Have I made any spelling and punctuation errors or omissions? (If there are certain mistakes that you often make, e.g. writing 'stoping' instead of 'stopping', then be on the look-out for these.)
- Have I punctuated my answers correctly? (Look for errors such as using repeated commas rather than full stops.)

TOP TIP

Don't leave gaps and always have a guess.

TOP TIP

Examiners are particularly unimpressed by words being incorrectly copied from the paper.

Multiple choice papers

Some schools set a **multiple choice comprehension paper**. This set out the passage in the normal way but follows it with questions to which you are offered a choice of answers. You then have to **circle** or **underli** the correct one. Again, it is vital not to leave any question unanswered.

There may also be some questions on the paper that require longer, writ answers.

See pages 72–73 for an example of a multiple choice paper. Your teacher you with more multiple choice papers to try.

ESSAYS

As part of the English exam you may be asked to write an **essay**. If your exam does include an essay, you will be given a choice of titles and styles such as:

- a story
- a description
- a letter
- a persuasive/argumentative/discussion piece.

Note that the essay you choose to write may include more than one of the styles of writing listed above.

> For example:
> - a letter may be a persuasive piece of writing
> - a story is likely to include some description
> - your response to a picture could be to write a story, a description, a letter or a persuasive piece.

Alternatively, you may be given a sentence which you have to use as the beginning of a piece of writing or you may have the option of continuing the passage used in the comprehension.

You will be given a fixed amount of **time** in which to write this essay and therefore you need to practise writing to a **time limit**. You need to make sure you can finish your essay in a way that satisfies you in that time. Different exams set different time limits, so it is worth checking how much time you will be given to write your essay.

TOP TIP
Try writing for 30 minutes, then 40 minutes, then 60 minutes at a time and see how much you can write. Then repeat the exercise and see if you can now write more in the same time.

Stories

How to write stories

PLANNING

In the time available to you in the exam, you will only be able to write a short story. Your story should therefore:

- have one basic idea – the action of the story should all be part of one main event
- have a small number of characters
- take place in one location
- take place over a short space of time, i.e. not have a series of paragraphs that begin, 'The next day…' or 'Three weeks later…'
- be as simple as possible.

TOP TIP
Complicated stories with lots of episodes or characters do not work well in a page or two of writing, and won't show how well you can write.

You may find it useful to think of writing a story as being like a train journey. A train driver leaves his home station knowing which stations he must go through in order to get to the final station. His whole journey is aimed towards that final destination. If he is not clear what the final destination is, he may well find himself going off in the wrong direction or being derailed and not knowing where he is or how to get back on track.

It is exactly the same with telling a story:

- The title may immediately give you an idea and you may be able to write the story through to the end without a problem.

- Or you may only be able to see the departure platform of your story and have no clear idea of where the story is going and what will need to happen on the way.

It helps to spend a few minutes thinking about your story:

- How *could* it end?
- What needs to happen to lead up to that end?
- What characters could get on or off?
- Will there be a delay, a problem that holds up the story train and needs to be resolved?
- What can be seen on the way? Is there some interesting description you can put in to help your reader imagine the story as you see it?

All stories need some sort of **problem** – or **conflict** – at their heart. Just as there may be a problem during a train journey – a tree on the line, the arrival of a robber, a signal failure – a story needs a problem and then a **solution**.

It also helps to think about what you would enjoy reading. If the title is 'A Party', would you enjoy reading a list of who came, what the presents were, what was eaten and what games were played? Or would you prefer to read a lively story about who spilled their drink over whom, who had a fight, a very surprising present or an unexpected guest? Might a story about preparing for the party or clearing up afterwards be more interesting?

When you are ready, jot down a **brief plan**. This will help you to organise your thoughts and keep you focused on the title.

1 THE TITLE

You may be writing your story in response to a **title**, a **picture** or a **sentence** that has to appear at some point in the story. If you are building your story around a title, it is particularly important that you do not lose sight of the title you have been given.

> For example, if your title is 'The Whistle' it is no good writing a story about a birthday visit to the zoo and tagging on a final sentence about how one friend gave you a whistle. Likewise, it is no good starting with 'Ben was given a beautiful silver whistle for his birthday' and then continuing with a saga about Ben's visit to the zoo with no further mention of the whistle.

2 FIRST OR THIRD PERSON

A story written from the **point of view** of the **writer** is written in the **first person**, e.g.:

- I went to school feeling gloomy and Mrs Hobbs made it worse by giving me low marks.

Stories in the **third person** are written about *he*, *she*, *it* or *they*. The same story in the third person might read:

- Laura went to school feeling gloomy and Mrs Hobbs made it worse by giving her low marks.

Your choice of first or third person can make a real difference to your story. If you write in the *first* person then you, as the narrator, know all about the central character and what he or she feels and does. If you are a *third* person narrator then you know about all the characters equally – although you can, of course, concentrate on one central character and go into much more detail about him or her.

We don't tend to write stories in the second person, e.g. '*You* went to school feeling gloomy and Mrs Hobbs made it worse by giving *you* one out of ten for *your* story' as it would sound very odd.

Look at the essay titles on page 45 and think about how you might write a story on any of them in the first person or the third person.

Look at your own books at home and see which are written in the first and which in the third person.

❸ WHERE TO START

You want to **grab your reader's attention** right at the start of your story. So, don't start with loads of detail about the main character's parents, siblings, home, neighbours and pets:

● My name is Sarah. I live in a house with my mother and father, my little brother Sam, my hamster, two budgies and my goldfish who is called Goldie…

Begin instead with something that will ensure your reader is interested from the start:

● Natasha finished eating the trainers and looked around for dessert. Mr Snooks had left his newspaper on the bird table but newspapers always tasted rusty and she fancied something sweet and syrupy. She slid off the bonnet of Mr Snooks' car and looked over the fence. The neighbours' children had gone inside and no-one was minding the roses. Natasha stretched her long neck over the fence and buried her nose in a cluster of Archduke Charles. A bit spiky but delicious!

TOP TIP
Once you are clear what your story is about, you can start in the middle and go back to fill in the details later, if they are needed.

❹ WHERE TO END

If you have **planned** your story properly, you won't have to panic two-thirds of the way through when you realise you don't know where you are going. You will also avoid an escape ending: 'then Sarah woke up. It had all been a dream!' And you will have an ending that fits with the beginning of the story and its title. Ideally, an ending should come naturally out of the story you have told up to that point. Clever story-tellers will enjoy **surprising** a reader.

For example, a story called 'The Precious Bowl' which involves Sarah using a precious bowl to put popcorn in while enjoying an evening in front of the TV, will *not* end with the breaking of the bowl but with Sarah breaking her leg as she balances on a chair to replace the bowl on the shelf. You can have fun surprising the reader's expectations in this way.

It is all right to leave the reader in some doubt about how things will end. You don't need to tell the reader every detail of the characters' future lives. Stories can end: '… as we walked back into the classroom, we wondered what on earth Mr Baggins would do next!' or 'Patterson put the ticket back into his pocket. He didn't want to use it but at least he knew it was there.'

TOP TIP
The end of your essay should be a believable conclusion to the story.

Story writing practice

When asked to write a story, is your response always: 'I can't think of anything to write'? Here are some ideas that will help you to start writing. The more practice you do, the easier it will become. Take some time to plan your story and write down a few notes. Then give yourself a time limit in which to write your story.

OBJECTS

You can make a story out of anything. You can write a hundred stories based on one simple object.

Collect three or four household objects, such as a pen, an apple, a plate, a bell, a candlestick. Look at each one in turn. See if you can think up a simple story about each one.

Here are some ideas for 'The Pen':

- A boy buys a pen and takes it to the park where he sits on a bench and writes a letter to his girlfriend. The pen drops out of his pocket and under the bench when he takes the letter to the post box. The next day the girl brings the letter to the park to read. She spots the pen under the bench and uses it to write her reply.

- Tom takes a new pen to school. It is borrowed by Oliver to write his homework and then lent to Ali to copy out his spellings and passed to Mrs Hobbs to correct the Maths test and ends up with Rhys, who draws a dinosaur, before Tom gets it back at the end of the day and finds it has quite run out.

> **TOP TIP**
> Keep practising – just for 15 minutes or so at a time – and you will find that the ideas start to come more easily. It can be fun seeing familiar objects in a new light.

Here are some ideas for 'The Candlestick':

- An old man likes to read by the light of a candle on a saucer. His daughter worries because the candle often falls over. One day, in exasperation, she comes home with a candlestick only to find her father happily reading by the light of an electric lamp.

- A woman on her way home from work spots an unusual candlestick in the window of the local antique shop. She takes a fancy to it, buys it, takes it home, unwraps it and puts it on the kitchen table. She hears her husband coming in and calling out, 'Look what I found in an antique shop on the way home!' He comes in and unwraps an identical candlestick to the one on the table.

PICTURES

Your parents might have made a **postcard collection** to help you with story ideas. Ask them to give you a choice of six cards and then choose your favourite. Write a story based on the picture.

If you haven't got a postcard collection then try finding pictures in **newspapers** and **magazines** which inspire you to write and use those instead.

Some exams ask you to write your essay in response to a picture so this is particularly good practice for that sort of essay.

Here are some postcards for you to practise with.

Ask an adult or friend to provide the 'bones' of a story – four to six points. Then use your imagination to fill in the detail – put on the 'flesh'.

Build a story around one of these skeletons:

- Dad opens the front door. A small dog is there. Dad brings it in. Dog eats meal. Then eats newspaper, carpet, shoes. Dad goes to put dog back outside door. Woman outside asks, 'Have you seen my dog?'

- Man chops down tree as it blocks light. Next day, garden full of birds squawking angrily at him. Squawking goes on into the night and next day. In desperation, man goes out and buys new tree.

- New boy in class – no one takes any notice of him. Teacher mentions that his father is a famous footballer/pop star/soap actor – everyone wants to be his friend.

- Woman on a bus finds a lost handbag. She searches for the owner and then takes it to police station. She realises she has left her own bag on the bus.

TOP TIP

You may not need to write notes for these stories as you have been given the outline.

Ask an adult or friend to give you the following: a character's name, a time or date, a setting, an object and one sentence which must appear in the story. Now see how many different stories you can write using these starting points.

STORY TITLES

Here are some story titles to try. Work towards writing the story in the time you will be given in the exam.

TOP TIP

Keep a clock or watch in sight while you work.

The Escape	The Nightmare Journey
A Day in the Country	Lost on the Underground
A Walk in the Woods	The Mysterious Chair
The Terribly Important Message	The Coach Trip
The Lost Guinea Pig	The Party
Trapped	The Best/Worst Present
The Race	A Terrible Fight
Going Shopping	The Storm
The Lost Dog	The Day I Climbed to the Top
Flying	Going for a Drive
Trick or Treat	Swimming
The Prisoner	Under the Pavement
The Day I Drove a Bus	The Shed
Dancing	Lost in a Crowd
A Horrible Dream	The Ancient Tree
The Junk Shop	Visiting
The New Headmaster	Broken Glass
The Key	The Magic Paint-box
My Favourite Shop	The Spotted Gringehopper
The New House	My Hero
A Dangerous Journey	The Repair Man
A School Trip	My New Machine
A Very Unusual Teacher	

One of the essay choices may be to write a story that begins with or includes a sentence or two that you are given. These can be quite fun – especially if you try not to write an obvious continuation. As with any kind of story, you do need to take the time to plan your story before you start.

Continue the story from these opening lines:

- I slammed the door of my room and threw myself onto my bed. I would have to do something and fast …

- I had never before broken a promise. This time, however, I had no choice …

- I had been swimming for several hours after the ship went down and was getting very tired when, suddenly, I saw land …

- There it was again. The creaking that had woken me up. And was that a light under the door …?

Descriptions

How to write descriptions

DESCRIBE THE DETAILS

Description should enable the reader to **picture** what you want them to **imagine**. Read these two different versions of a story called 'The Picnic':

- Karim and Naveen went for a picnic. They went to the park and met James and Richard there. They decided to play cricket before eating the picnic. The park was full of people. Then a dog came and ran off with their ball. They chased the dog all over the park and round the pond. Then the dog jumped into the pond and dropped the ball. He then came out and shook himself all over the boys. Naveen got very cross but Karim laughed and dropped the picnic. The dog jumped on the sandwiches and ate them.

- It was a bright, breezy day so Karim and Naveen decided to go for a picnic. They quickly slapped together all their favourite sandwiches – peanut butter with marmite, honey and pickle, and egg and strawberry jam. Karim had to stop Naveen stuffing most of them into his mouth as he wrapped them up! They gathered their cricket bats and a ball and strolled down to the park  where they bumped into James and Richard. They agreed to play cricket first and have the picnic afterwards. Suddenly, James hit a ball into the bushes and a large black and white dog raced in after it. He charged off to the other side of the park with all the boys galloping after him, yelling and waving their bats. The dog was having a lovely time and ended up by jumping into the pond, dropping the ball and laughing at them. He then came out and shook himself energetically, drenching the boys. Naveen was furious but Karim laughed so much that he dropped the picnic. The dog was delighted, jumped on the sandwiches and gobbled them up.

The first extract is dull, whereas the second extract gives you details about the weather, the place, the characters and the atmosphere.

Write a few sentences of description of people or places you know. Add details – and even a little exaggeration – to bring what you are describing to life.

USE YOUR SENSES

By using your **five senses** – seeing, hearing, smelling, tasting and touching – you can give the reader a real sense of what it is you are describing.

Practise describing foods in terms of their shape, smell, taste and feel. Think about the details and really stretch your vocabulary. Choose from the following:

- an egg
- a slice of bread
- a chocolate bar
- a cornflake.

TOP TIP

You could play this as a game. For example, describe a banana and ask the other members of your team to guess what the object is.

USE YOUR IMAGINATION

The following exercises will help you to write **detailed descriptions**. You are asked to put yourself in unusual situations and think about what you would experience if you were there. These exercises will stretch your imagination and vocabulary too!

The beetle in the fridge

Imagine you are a beetle stranded in your family fridge. The beetle has to find its way around the bread, eggs, milk, cheese, cream, vegetables, fruit, etc. Think about what these things would feel like for a beetle and what dangers there might be – drowning in a tub of cream, sliding down an eggshell. Write from the beetle's point of view – and concentrate on the detail.

The spider in the corner

Imagine that a spider has made its web in a top corner of your bedroom. Think about what it could see from there, whether its view is interrupted by a cupboard or a chest of drawers, what your bed looks like from up there, what the room looks like when the door opens, what it hears and feels, what it understands of what it sees. Write about your own room from the spider's point of view and, again, think detail!

TOP TIP

If you enjoy doing this, try the spider's view of the classroom, an insect's view of your garden, a bee is trapped inside your car and so on.

Under my bed

Describe the space underneath your bed. You can either imagine a whole different world under there or describe it just as it is – old socks and all. Whichever you choose, make sure that your description includes lots of detail.

Writers like to help you picture what they are imagining. To do this, they often make **pictures in words**. They write about one thing as if it were something else.

> For example, Ted Hughes, in a poem called 'Esther's Tomcat', begins:
>
> Daylong this tomcat lies stretched flat
> As an old rough mat, no mouth and no eyes.
>
> This helps us to picture a battered old cat lying asleep.
>
> In the next example, an extract from a short poem called 'The Embankment', TE Hulme, writing from the point of view of a homeless person, cold on the streets at night, asks God to:
>
> … make small
> The old star-eaten blanket of the sky,
> That I may fold it round me and in comfort lie.
>
> This conjures up a vivid picture of the night sky as a comforting blanket for a cold and hungry person.

A **metaphor** is a comparison of one thing to another. A metaphor writes of one thing as if it is another thing, e.g. the sky *is* 'an old star-eaten blanket'.

A metaphor that makes a **direct comparison**, i.e. saying one thing is *like* something else or saying it is *as* something else – like Esther's cat and the doormat – is called a **simile**.

Here is an extract from a famous description of a smokey industrial town in the mid-nineteenth century. It is taken from *Hard Times* by Charles Dickens and contains pictures in words that bring a liveliness and imaginative quality to the description:

> It was a town of red brick, or of brick that would have been red if the smoke and ashes had allowed it; but as matters stood, it was a town of unnatural red and black like the painted face of a savage.
>
> It was a town of machinery and tall chimneys, out of which interminable serpents of smoke trailed themselves for ever and ever, and never got uncoiled.
>
> It had a black canal in it, and a river that ran purple with ill-smelling dye, and vast piles of buildings full of windows where there was a rattling and a trembling all day long, and where the piston of the steam-engine worked monotonously up and down, like the head of an elephant in a state of melancholy madness.

To do

Find two similes and a metaphor in the extract above.
See page 82 for some answers.

AIM HIGH

Personification is another kind of comparison, which involves writing about something that *isn't* a person as if it were.

> For example:
> - The wind in its fury raged round the house and screamed down the chimney.
> - Snow gently covered the cottage, nuzzling round it to keep it snug.
> - The old car coughed and spluttered as it limped up the hill.

This gives the objects character, enables the reader to picture what is being described and makes the writing more lively and interesting.

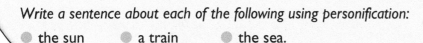

Write a sentence about each of the following using personification:
- the sun
- a train
- the sea.

USE THE SOUND OF WORDS

Our **sense of sound** is particularly important when it comes to creating **atmosphere** and a sense of being in a **particular place** or **situation**. The poet John Keats wrote a lovely poem about autumn called 'Ode to Autumn'. It begins with a sense of frantic activity when everyone is rushing around getting the harvest in.

For example, this includes the bees that have more pollen and nectar to collect than they know what to do with:

> For summer has o'erbrimm'd their clammy cells.

Keats has used three lots of double 'm' in this line to imitate the gentle humming of the busy bees. This use of word sound to imitate a real sound is called **onomatopoeia**.

TOP TIP

If you are writing about something that makes a noise, try to imitate the sound with the words you use.

You could use the following words to describe bath water running: gurgling, glugging, sploshing, splashing. Think of some onomatopoeic words to describe:

- a stream
- the wind in trees
- a car starting
- waves crashing onto a pebbly beach.

Alliteration creates an effect by repeating (usually) the first letters or sounds of words. It can be used to imitate a real life sound – as with onomatopoeia – or to make a saying more memorable. It is often used in speeches and lots of famous proverbs also rely on alliteration.

For example:
- Time and tide wait for no man.
- Waste not, want not.
- Practice makes perfect.

Try making up some alliterative phrases to:

- imitate a sound, e.g. the wind in leaves, the stroke of a paintbrush on a canvas, a storm at sea, a drummer drumming
- make a memorable saying, e.g. about punctuality, friendship, hunger, money.

Assonance is the repetition of the vowel sounds in a word.

For example, here is that line from Keats's 'Ode to Autumn' again – this time with the lines just before it. The repeated sounds of long vowels in the underlined words give a sense of the richness of heavy flowers with all the pollen and scent the bees are so busily collecting:

> ....to set budding <u>more</u>,
> And still <u>more</u>, later <u>flowers</u> for the <u>bees</u>,
> Until they think <u>warm days</u> will never <u>cease</u>,
> For Summer has <u>o'erbrimmed</u> their clammy cells.

The personification of Autumn is being busy, rushing around.

AIM HIGH

Long vowels are the sounds that are made when you say the letters by name:
- 'a' as in 'make', 'e' as in 'seed', 'i' as in 'eye', 'o' as in 'fold' and 'u' as in 'fuel'.

Short vowels are:
- 'a' as in 'pack', 'e' as in 'egg', 'i' as in 'pick', 'o' as in 'dog' and 'u' as in 'fluff'.

Try making up some lines in which assonance helps to create an atmosphere or particular sounds, such as those:

- in a zoo at night
- on a motorway
- in a busy kitchen
- in an office where lots of people are tapping away on keyboards.

Descriptive writing practice

ADDING DESCRIPTIONS

Here is a piece of lifeless writing. Try to enliven it by adding descriptive detail, choosing more interesting words and, perhaps, using your senses to help.

> It was a nice day so instead of taking the bus I decided to walk to my grandmother's. I put some things for her into a basket. I went out of the gate. I walked to the park and crossed the field. I went down the alley that leads to the woods. I saw lots of trees and small animals. The sun was warm. I heard some unusual noises. I looked round. I could see grandma's house through the woods. I opened her door. Grandma was in bed. She looked different. I offered her some cake. She looked hungry. 'What big eyes you have, grandma,' I said.

WRITING DESCRIPTIONS

Using some of the skills you have been practising, write descriptions (not stories) of:

- Learning to swim
- Walking home in the rain
- Eating spaghetti
- A very old person
- A baby
- An expensive piece of jewellery
- A dark night
- A restaurant kitchen
- Your room from the point of view of one of your toys.

ESSAY TITLES

Here are some more descriptions to try. Work towards writing the description in the time you will be given in the exam.

- My life in 2030
- My grandmother
- An old building or old object
- A place I know well
- If I had my own shop…
- A job I would like to do
- My favourite food

How to write letters – formal and informal

Letters can be to people you know, thank-you letters or fan letters, or they can be letters to organisations, e.g. newspapers on a particular topic, letters of complaint to a shop or a company. It is important to know how such letters are set out and the differences between thanking your aunt for the book-token and asking the BBC to do a programme on hang-gliding.

Here is a formal letter. It is set out in a formal, organised way.

> 17 Doghouse Road
> Howling
> Wintershire
> W0E 5ME
>
> The Manager
> Tragedy Holidays
> Cloudy Bay
> Darkshire
> S0 BAD
>
> 20th August 2012
>
> Dear Sir
>
> We have just returned from the holiday on the island of Lousirotti which we booked with you. It was a disaster. Your representative, who met us at the airport, was two hours late and then took us to the wrong hotel. We had booked rooms with sea views but our rooms faced the car park and, in any case, the sea was so far away we could hardly see it from the front of the hotel. We were given the same food every evening except for Thursday when we had apple crumble instead of apple tart. The children's entertainer was so frightening that our children had nightmares and screamed every time he appeared.
>
> In all, this was nothing like the holiday described in your brochure. We look forward to your response to our complaint and we expect an immediate refund of our payment.
>
> Yours faithfully
>
> Mr and Mrs U N Rested

Here is a much less formal letter. The style is more relaxed and more conversational.

> 17 Prickle Close
> Gorse Bush
> Thornley
> Bristle
> OUC H11
>
> 21st June 2012
>
> Dear Mary and Nick
>
> Thank you so much for having me over last weekend. I had a brilliant time and I won't forget the meringues for ages. I have downloaded a recipe from the internet and am going to try to make them myself but they won't be as good.
>
> It was great playing with Tom and Jack and mum has already mended the rip in my shorts that Jack made so don't worry. I'd love Jack to stay with us when you go away but dad says he doesn't want Jack digging up the garden and I don't see how we could stop him! It might be better if Tom stays instead – Dad likes dogs! And Jack can always look after the garden in your French house, can't he?
>
> I hope you all have a great holiday. Thanks again.
>
> Love from Ben

It is important to choose just the **right words** to suit the **purpose** of the letter and the person to whom you are writing:

● As with all kinds of writing, your aim is to be clear and straightforward.

● You will be formal with official letters or letters to people you don't know personally and more relaxed with family or friends.

● Some people think they have to dress up letters in grand language but this is never necessary.

Letter writing practice

THE RIGHT WORDS

Here is a letter with various places where you have a choice of words. In each case, choose the expression you feel is best in the context:

The Manager
Flickey Mouse Cinema
Still Street
Oscarham
Hollyshire
                                                                    30th July

Dear Sir

Your programme for the next season of films has (just arrived/just plopped onto my doormat/just become available to me). I (notice/am aware/spot) that once again there are no films for children in your programme. My friends and I love films and we (think it's well cool when we go on/really enjoy/take immense pleasure in) our trips to your cinema but it feels as if you (don't regard our preferences with any degree of importance/don't give a monkey's about us/don't take us into consideration) when you plan your programme. Children's films can be (very good/of exceptional quality/wicked) and I'm sure you would attract good audiences if you put them on. I would like to (twist your arm/encourage you/persuade you) to include some films for younger people when you plan your next season. (After all/May I remind you/I mean) you are developing your audiences for the future.

(Yours sincerely/Goodbye/That's all for now)

D V Dee-Fan

ESSAY TITLES

Here are some letters to try. Work towards writing the letter in the time you will be given in the exam.

Write a letter to:

● someone you admire, asking for their autograph

● your new neighbour, apologising for driving your bike into their car

● your best friend, who is moving from another part of the country to live near you

● the Prime Minister, explaining why your school should – or should not – be knocked down to build a new one.

TOP TIP

Keep a clock or watch in sight while you work.

How to write a persuasive/argumentative/discussion piece

BE PERSUASIVE

Much writing in everyday life is aimed at **persuading** people. Politicians write speeches to persuade people to vote for them or to see things as they do. Religious leaders, union leaders, charity directors and sales staff all need to persuade people to see things in their way. And you need to persuade people too. Perhaps you want your parents to let you have a sleepover, or go on holiday, start learning an instrument or stop learning an instrument.

A successful persuasion is one that bears two things in mind from the start:

- what you want to achieve
- how the person you want to persuade is going to feel about it.

Nagging usually achieves the opposite of what you want – everyone hates being nagged. Try to see the issue from the point of view of the person you want to persuade.

For example, here is Laura's mum persuading Laura to tidy her room:

Start by seeming to be on the same side as the person you want to persuade.

Darling, it will be so nice when Sarah comes to stay next weekend. It's ages since you had a sleepover, isn't it? I wonder how you will manage to fit her into your room – or were you thinking she might sleep on the stairs? That might be a bit tricky if Bounder comes up in the night – you know what he's like! Does Sarah mind her face being licked? Of course, you might think of moving – just a little – some of the things in your room? I mean, I realise it's all very precious – especially all that wrapping paper left after your birthday in the summer. I could – I mean, if you didn't mind – take it downstairs for you if you could just pick it off your floor? And, I suppose you might even find your watch under there somewhere – do you think? And I've often wondered whether my scissors could have found their way in there somehow? It might be quite fun to look!

Sound as reasonable as you can.

Anticipate the kind of objections that might be made to what you want.

Offer little bribes, e.g. If I do this would you do that?

To do

Try writing a letter of persuasion to:

- your local MP, asking him or her to support the building of a new sports centre in your area
- your grandparents, asking them if you can come and stay during the holidays
- your parents, asking them if you can have a sleepover.

TOP TIP

Successful persuasion depends on picking the right moment, a good argument and finding the right language.

Sometimes, interesting questions come up on which one can see two – or more – **points of view**. A question can be discussed from **various angles** – without taking up a particular **standpoint**. It can help to imagine how different people with different opinions might consider a question.

> For example, let's take the question of school uniform. Imagine that a new school is opening and there is a discussion as to whether or not to have compulsory uniform. The following points might be made by teachers with differing views:
>
> ● uniform makes life easier for the pupils – no decision on what to wear first thing each morning
>
> ● uniform equalises people – it means that everyone wears the same and no-one can show off their clothes because they have more money than someone else
>
> ● uniform is quite expensive compared to ordinary clothes and it's unfair to make it compulsory
>
> ● uniform makes it easy for teachers who take school trips to spot their pupils in a crowd
>
> ● uniform is sensible – shirts, sweatshirts, trousers or skirts – it stops pupils wearing unsuitable clothes to school, e.g. crop tops
>
> ● uniform is smart – it makes the pupils take pride in their appearance
>
> ● uniform rules are hard to enforce – it gives the teachers a lot of additional and irritating work.

To do

Imagine you are the headteacher of the new school. Use the points above to discuss the question of whether or not school uniform should be compulsory in the school. You may also bring in new points of your own. You may, if you like, come to a decision at the end or you can leave the question open.

Persuasive/argumentative/discussion writing practice

PREPARE YOUR ARGUMENT

Imagine you are desperate to have a dog. Your parents have always said no. They might say:

● You won't look after it properly.

● Dogs are a tie and make it hard to go away.

● Dogs need walks and you are lazy.

How could you argue against these points?

● It will be good for me to learn responsibility.

● I will research good local kennels.

● I will get an alarm clock and walk the dog before school.

And rather than go on and on to your parents, you might begin:

● Dad, Mum, is now a good time for us to have a little talk?

To do

Try finishing this persuasive piece.
Use the arguments provided above.

WRITING A DISCUSSION

Discuss the following questions in the manner of the school uniform discussion above. You may like to make a list of points – as above – before you write your discussion:

● School is for work and home is for relaxation. Homework should be banned until senior school.

● Schools do not do enough sport. Every afternoon should be spent in some kind of physical activity.

- The world still has terrible diseases and many hungry people. Until that is no longer true, we should not give money to animal charities.
- All zoos should be closed.

ESSAY TITLES

Here are some persuasive/argumentative/discussion pieces to try. Work towards writing the piece in the time you will be given in the exam.

- Questions I should like to ask the Loch Ness Monster.
- What I *don't* want to be when I grow up.
- If I were Prime Minister for a day…
- Children should never be smacked – do you agree?
- Why I do/don't think television is a good thing.
- Why I would (not) like to be an only child.

TOP TIP
Keep a clock or watch in sight while you work.

Checking

As with your comprehension answers, your essay should ideally be **checked twice**.

On the **first read-through** ask yourself the following:

- Have I written what I meant to write throughout?
- Is what I have written clear?
- Is what I have written sufficiently detailed?
- Is what I have written sufficiently explanatory?
- Do I repeat myself?
- Have I contradicted myself? (For example, is Ben taller than Luke at the start of the story but shorter by the end?)

On the **second read-through** ask yourself the following:

- Is the spelling and punctuation all correct? (Pay particular attention to mistakes you know are your weak points.)

TOP TIP
Remember to leave time for checking. If you finish early check, check and check again!

EXAM PRACTICE

This section includes **12 comprehension exercises**. Two are **practice papers** and are laid out like **exam papers** (see pages 68–72). The last one is a **multiple choice** comprehension (see pages 72–73).

The first comprehension is a good **assessment exercise** (see page 56) to do with an adult. The following eight comprehensions then get a little more challenging and include some **aim high** material to help **stretch** and **develop** your skills further. The last exercise, following the practice papers, is an example of a multiple choice comprehension.

The passages cover a range of types of writing – fiction and fact, simple and more complex language, prose and verse.

TOP TIP
Remember to read the questions as carefully as the passage. More marks are lost through inaccurate reading of the questions than anything else.

Each comprehension question is given a mark and roughly how long the comprehension should take. Remember to divide your time according to what each question is worth. Read the passage *carefully*. Look through the questions then read the passage carefully again. Then – off you go! Write your answers in full sentences (see page 39 for tips about how to do this.)

Suggested answers are at the end of the book but try not to look at them until you have had a good try at the exercise.

Each comprehension exercise, apart from the first and last one, is followed by a choice of essay titles. The first four essays give you a chance to warm up but after that a suggested time limit is given. You could then do the first four again, this time giving yourself a time limit.

Pinched Legs! NR

Whoo! Emil jumped. He had nearly fallen asleep, and that would never do. He wished someone else would get in, so that he would not be alone with Bowler-hat, but no-one did, though the train stopped at several stations. It was still only four o'clock, so there was more than two hours to go before they reached Berlin. He tried pinching his legs, as that always helped to keep him awake during history   5
lessons at school. Then he began to wonder what his cousin Pony looked like now, for he could not really remember her face at all. He only knew that when Grandma and Aunt Martha had brought her to Neustadt – oh, a long time ago – Pony had wanted to fight him. Of course he had refused. She was no more than flyweight then, to his welterweight, so it would have been quite unfair, and he had told her so.   10
Why if he'd given her one of his uppercuts, they'd have had to scrape what was left of her off the wall! But she had kept on and on about it, until her mother got tired of it, and made her stop.

Ough! He was nodding again, and had nearly rolled off the seat. He pinched himself and dug his fingers into his legs until he was sure they must be black and blue,   15
but it didn't seem to do a bit of good. He tried counting the buttons on the seat opposite. Counted one way there were twenty-four, counted the other, he could not make more than twenty-three. He leaned back, wondering why that was – and so fell sound asleep.

Emil and The Detectives, Erich Kastner

Questions

So he would not be alone with Bowler Hat on a train

1. Where is Emil during this passage? ~~at the train station~~ (2)
2. Why did he 'jump' in the first sentence? because he fell asleep (2)
3. Why did Emil hope someone else would get in? so he wouldn't do the job (2)
4. Does Emil enjoy his history lessons? How do you know? yes because that always helped to keep him awake during history lessons at school (3)
5. Why do you think Emil had refused to fight Pony? She was no more than flyweight (3)
6. Give two methods Emil uses to try to avoid falling asleep. he pinched himself and dug his fingers into his until he was sure they must be (2)
7. Can you think up any other things he might have tried? You will need at least two. black and blue. (4)
8. Write a paragraph about a time when you:

   a) tried to keep awake

   or

   b) tried to fall asleep.

   You should write at least five lines. (7)

Time: 30 minutes   **Total marks available: 25**

During the test at school, I didn't have to do the test only the other children. When I was reading my book, I fell asleep, but woke up again and fell asleep and when the timer went off, I woke straight back up and I wasn't tired again.

Banana Man

In 1878, the 2nd Lord Leconfield of Petworth House, in West Sussex, sent his gardener to Kew to learn how to grow a banana tree. He had been told that bananas tasted better straight from the tree. All the necessary **paraphernalia**, including a special greenhouse, was installed at Petworth. What followed is recounted by his grandson:

"The banana tree was splendid. My grandfather took a lively interest in its progress until, lo and behold, it **fructified**. 'I will have that banana for dinner tonight,' he said, as soon as the banana was ripe. And so he did – amid a deathly hush. All were agog.   5

The banana was brought in on a **lordly** dish. My grandfather peeled it with a golden knife. He then cut a sliver off and, with a golden fork, put it in his mouth and carefully tasted it. Whereupon he flung dish, plate, knife, fork and banana onto the floor and shouted,   10
'Oh God, it tastes just like any other damn banana!' Banana tree and all were ordered to be destroyed. My famous old gardener told me that the banana cost my grandfather some £3000."

National Trust Magazine, Summer 1998

Questions

1. Who was sent to Kew to learn about growing bananas?   (1)
2. Why did Lord Leconfield want a banana tree?   (2)
3. 'My grandfather took a lively interest' in the tree, says the writer in l.5 (but he doesn't tell us *how* he might have shown this interest). What do you think Lord Leconfield might have done to show his interest in the tree while it was growing?   (3)
4. What was the atmosphere like before Lord Leconfield began to eat the banana? Try to describe it in some detail.   (3)
5. What happened when he tasted the banana?   (3)
6. Why does the writer say that the banana 'cost my grandfather some £3000.' In today's money that would probably be more like £3,000,000. What might have made it so expensive?   (3)
7. What do you think the following words mean? They are in bold print in the passage:
   a) paraphernalia (l.3)   (2)
   b) fructified (l.6)   (2)
   c) lordly (l.8)   (2)
8. What sort of character do you think Lord Leconfield was?   (4)

   Time: 25 minutes   **Total marks available: 25**

Essay

a) You are Lord Leconfield's gardener on the day after the banana tasting incident. Write a letter home to your parents telling them what happened. Make sure you describe not just the incident itself but your feelings about the whole episode. Remember to write *appropriately* i.e. this is not a formal letter but a family one.

b) You are very keen to have a bit of garden for yourself. Imagine you have to prepare your arguments so that you can persuade your parents. Write it as a letter – perhaps you can imagine they are on holiday and you want them to think about it while they are away. Remember to think about their point of view and how you can argue against what they might say.

Gathering Leaves

Spades take up leaves
No better than spoons,
And bags full of leaves
Are light as balloons.

I make a great noise
Of rustling all day
Like rabbit and deer
Running away.

But the mountains I raise
Elude my embrace,
Flowing over my arms
And into my face.

I may load and unload
Again and again
Till I fill the whole shed,
And what have I then?

Next to nothing for weight,
And since they grew duller
From contact with earth,
Next to nothing for colour.

Next to nothing for use.
But a crop is a crop,
And who's to say where
The harvest shall stop?

Robert Frost

Questions

1. What job is the writer trying to do in the first verse? What two things is he using? (2)

2. What comparison is he making in the second verse? (2)

3. What problem do you think he is having in the first two lines? (2)

4. Can you find one simile and one metaphor in the poem? (2)

5. What is he trying to do in the third verse? What problem is he having? (2)

6. In the fifth and sixth verses he repeats the phrase 'next to nothing'. What is this referring to? (3)

7. What do you understand by the last verse? (3)

8. The poem is about the gathering of leaves in the autumn. What impression do you get of the man who is doing this? What about the language of the poem? **AIM HIGH** (3)

9. Write *a paragraph* on one of the following three examples:
   a) a tree or a wood in the spring
   or
   b) a tree or a wood in the autumn

or

c) a tree or a wood in the winter.

You may write descriptively or give an account of an incident – whichever you choose.   (6)

Time: 35 minutes   **Total marks available: 25**

Essay

Write about one of the following:

a)   A job I don't like doing

b)   The Garden

c)   Why I do/don't prefer to play outside

Buffalo Halt

AIM HIGH *This extract comes from a famous story about a man who – in the age before aeroplanes, fast trains and cars – made a bet that he could go around the world in only 80 days. He has many delays and mishaps on the way. Here we learn about one of them.*

After lunch, Mr Fogg, Mrs Aouda and their companions went back to their comfortable seats in the carriage and settled down to watch the varied scenery that passed before their eyes – vast prairies, mountains outlined against the horizon, creeks tumbling and foaming on their way. Sometimes, a great herd of buffalo would gather in the distance, looking like a moving dam. Huge armies of these ruminants* frequently pose an insurmountable barrier to the progress of a train on its journey. One can watch the animals in their thousands filing past in serried ranks for hours and hours, across the railway tracks. The engine is forced to stop and wait till the line is clear again.   5

That is exactly what happened on this occasion. At about three o'clock in the afternoon, a herd of ten or twelve thousand buffalo blocked the line. After slowing down, the engine driver tried to push his buffers through the side of the immense column of animals but he had to stop in the face of this impenetrable mass.   10

Everyone watched as the ruminants* marched peacefully by, occasionally bellowing noisily. They were larger than European bulls but had short legs and short tails, widely spaced horns and long manes which covered their muscular humps. There was no point in trying to stop such a migration. When buffaloes have set off in a particular direction, nothing can divert them or get them to change their course. They are a torrent of living flesh which no dam can hold back.   15   20

The travellers watched this curious sight from the platforms. But the one to whom the loss of time was most serious, Mr Phileas Fogg, stayed in his seat and waited philosophically till the buffaloes should be pleased to move out of the way. Passepartout was furious at the delay caused by this great collection of animals and was eager to take shots at them with his arsenal of revolvers.   25

"What a country!" he exclaimed, "where mere cows can stop trains and plod along in a procession, not remotely hurrying themselves, and not caring in the least that they are stopping the traffic! For goodness sake! I should very much like to know whether Mr Fogg made provision for this hold-up in his schedule! And what a useless engine driver who hasn't got the nerve to drive his engine through these obstructive beasts!"   30

The engine driver certainly hadn't attempted to drive through the obstruction and had behaved very sensibly. The buffers would, no doubt, have

crushed the first buffaloes but, powerful though it was, the engine would have
had to stop eventually, the train would have been derailed and would have been
left lying helpless by the wayside.

The only thing to do was to wait patiently and hope to make up the lost
time by greater acceleration as soon as they could restart the train. The
buffaloes' march-past lasted three long hours and it was nightfall by the time
the line was clear again. At the moment when the last of the herd were crossing
the rails, the first were disappearing over the horizon.

Around the World in Eighty Days, Jules Verne

* *ruminants* are hoofed animals which live by chewing their food over and over again

Questions

1. Where are Mr Fogg and Mrs Aouda sitting at the start of the passage? (2)

2. The writer says the travellers watched 'the varied scenery that passed before
their eyes' (ll.2–3) but scenery doesn't move! What do you understand by this
sentence? (3)

3. What problem is caused by the herd of buffalo? (2)

4. Why was there no point in trying to stop the migration? (2)

5. What is surprising about Mr Fogg's reaction to the delay? Why is it surprising? (3)

6. What sort of person might Passepartout be? Describe his character using the
evidence in the passage. (3)

7. In what way do you think the engine driver behaved 'very sensibly'? (3)

8. Was the time spent waiting for the buffaloes lost forever or was there something
the driver could do to make up the time? (2)

9. Describe in your own words and as fully as possible what the passengers could
see after their long wait was nearly over. (5)

Time: 35 minutes   **Total marks available: 25**

Essay

a) Imagine that you are the engine driver of this train. After a long day in which you were
delayed by the buffalo, you finally reach your night's lodging and write a letter home to your
family telling them about the day.

b) 'Punctuality is the politeness of Kings', is an old saying. How important do you think it is to be
on time?

c) Write about a time when you found it hard to be patient.

Life on Earth

The world must have seemed a very strange, empty place when the dinosaurs
had all gone. There were no other giant animals to take their place right away.
The forests and plains would have seemed very quiet. There were no flying
pterosaurs, or ichthyosaurs and plesiosaurs in the sea.

If you looked a little closer, though, you would have seen many animals still alive.   5
There were birds in the trees, crocodiles and turtles in the rivers and seas, frogs,
lizards, snakes, and small furry animals on the ground.

These furry animals were the mammals which had been around since Late Triassic
times. The mammals lived beneath the feet of the dinosaurs, but they were quite small,
generally no bigger than a mouse or a rat. During the Cretaceous period, some of the   10
mammals became larger, reaching the size of a cat, but they could never become really
large because the dinosaurs were around. When the dinosaurs had gone, the mammals
had their chance. In the first 10 million years of the Tertiary period, which came after
the Cretaceous, many new kinds of mammals appeared, like the first horses, bats, and
large plant-eaters.   15

The forests filled up rapidly. The early horses, and their relatives, were about the size
of terriers, and they fed on leaves. There were cat-like meat-eaters which fed on them.
In the trees above were climbing, insect-eating mammals, some of which were the
earliest relatives of monkeys and apes (and, of course, of humans).

On the open ground were some large plant-eating mammals, which were 4 metres   20
long, and 2 metres tall at the shoulders. Some of these forms had horns. It had not
taken long before the mammals replaced the dinosaurs!

By about 25 million years ago, in the middle of the Tertiary period, many
new forms of mammals had come on the scene: rabbits, elephants, camels, dogs,   25
bears, pigs and beavers. A big change had also taken place in the long-necked
camels. The largest plant-eaters were brontotheres and rhinoceroses. One of the
rhinoceroses reached a length of 8 metres and a height of 5 metres. A brontothere
looked rather like a rhinoceros, but it had a strange double horn on its nose which
looked like a catapult.   30

The Hamlyn Book of Dinosaurs, Michael Benton

Questions

1. The world 'must have seemed a very strange, empty place when the dinosaurs had
   all gone,' we are told in the first paragraph. In what three different places would this
   have been noticeable? (3)

2. Was the world really empty? How do you know? (2)

3. What type of animal developed in new ways after the disappearance of the dinosaurs? (2)

4. In paragraph 4, three different kinds of animal diets are mentioned. What are they? (3)

5. Where did the largest animals live during the Tertiary period? (2)

6. What did our own earliest ancestors eat? (2)

7. What four facts can you find about a Brontothere? (4)

8. Three different pre-historic periods are mentioned in the passage. Find them and
   write them down in the order in which they occurred in real life. (3)

9. Many mammals are named in the passage. Give the names of as many as you can. (4)

Time: 40 minutes   **Total marks available: 25**

Essay

a) You have discovered an animal which had been thought to be extinct. Describe it in detail, informing your readers of its diet, habitat, appearance, the way it moves etc.

b) Write a review for your local paper of a meal you have had in a new local restaurant. Think about the service and the atmosphere in the restaurant as well as the food.

c) Does it matter if some animals become extinct? Write a speech you could make to your class arguing your point of view.

She lies by the Island of Spices and Zephyrs*

She lies by the Island of Spices and Zephyrs
where the monkeys play hide and seek up in old trees
and the humming-birds balance all day on a single
blade of tall grass as it sways in the breeze.

There the gold fish blow bubbles among water lilies
simply to pass the time of day
and high on the mountain the summer cloud lingers
rather than pass on its heavenly way.

She lies there and roses climb out of her portholes,
and juniper trails from her f'castle** down.
At her figurehead glitters the eye of the basilisk***
like the sea-green jewel of a gold crown.

She lies there, rock riven, her mizzen mast shattered
and the seaweeds garb her all over in green.
Who was she? Who knows? Who knows? No-one.
The name on her side will never be seen.

George Barker

* a zephyr is a gentle breeze
** the f'castle or 'forecastle' is the front of a ship; it is pronounced 'foke-sal'
*** a basilisk is a mythical reptile that could kill you with a look

Questions

1. Who is the 'she' mentioned in the first line?   (1)

2. a) What kind of atmosphere is George Barker describing in
       the first two verses?   (2)

    b) Would you like to visit this place? Give reasons for your feelings.   (2)

    3. The ship is referred to as 'she'. Can you find any other
        personifications in the poem?   (2)

4. The poem is full of examples of life in the natural world. Choose two and say why
    they appeal to you.   (3)

5. In the last verse there is an explanation and a question. Can you identify them both?   (4)

6. Imagine you know the truth of what happened to the 'she' in this poem. Tell the story
    from the point of view of someone who was there.   (6)

Time: 35 minutes   **Total marks available: 20**

Essay

Write a story about one of the following, trying to write as descriptively as possible. Spend about 30 minutes on this essay.

a)   The Shipwreck

b)   A Day in Paradise

c)   Life Under Water

Costume Drama

Eventually we reached the bay, spread out the rugs on the sand, arranged the food, placed the battalion of wine-bottles in a row in the shallows to keep cool, and the great moment had arrived. Amid much cheering Mother removed her housecoat and stood revealed in all her glory, clad in the bathing-costume which made her look, as Larry pointed out, like a sort of marine Albert Memorial. Roger behaved very well   5
until he saw Mother wade into the shallow water in a slow and dignified manner. He then got terribly excited. He seemed to be under the impression that the bathing costume was some sort of sea monster that had enveloped Mother and was now about to carry her out to sea. Barking wildly, he flung himself to the rescue, grabbed one of the frills dangling so plentifully round the edge of the costume, and tugged with   10
all his strength in order to pull Mother back to safety. Mother, who had just remarked that she thought the water a little cold, suddenly found herself being pulled backwards. With a squeak of dismay, she lost her footing and sat down heavily in two feet of water, while Roger tugged so hard that a large section of the frill gave way. Elated by the fact that the enemy appeared to be disintegrating, Roger, growling encouragement to Mother,   15
set to work to remove the rest of the offending monster from her person. We writhed on the sand, helpless with laughter, while Mother sat gasping in the shallows, making desperate attempts to regain her feet, beat Roger off, and retain at least a portion of her costume. Unfortunately, owing to the extreme thickness of the material from which the costume was constructed, the air was trapped inside; the effect of the water made it   20
inflate like a balloon, and trying to keep this airship of frills and tucks under control added to Mother's difficulties. In the end it was Theodore who shooed Roger away and helped Mother to her feet. Eventually, after we had partaken of a glass of wine to celebrate and recover from what Larry referred to as Perseus's rescue of Andromeda, we went in to swim, and Mother sat discreetly in the shallows, while Roger crouched   25
nearby, growling ominously at the costume as it bulged and fluttered round Mother's waist.

My Family and Other Animals, Gerald Durrell

Questions

1.	Suggest two reasons why the family had gone to the bay.	(2)
2.	What was 'the great moment' (l.3)?	(2)
3.	Why did Roger get 'terribly excited' (l.7)?	(2)
4.	Describe, as far as possible in your own words, Mother's costume. Look carefully!	(3)
5.	What happened to the costume when Mother was sitting in the water?	(2)
6.	Why do you think it took so long for anyone to help Mother?	(2)
7.	What impression do you get of Larry?	(2)

8. Imagine that you are either:

Mother

or

Roger

Give your version of what happened during this extract. (5)

9. Did you enjoy this passage? Explain why this piece of writing does or does not appeal to you, giving examples from the passage. (5)

Time: 40 minutes **Total marks available: 25**

Essay

Give an account of one of the following – firstly in the first person and then in the third. You should tell roughly the same story but your accounts may well differ in length. Spend about 30 minutes on this.

a) The Burglary

b) The Interview

c) A Family Day Out

Mecca

From time immemorial, Mecca has been a stopping place for travellers, maybe because of the well of Zamzam, which provided water in the mountainous desert landscape of western Arabia. At some time, a cube-shaped temple was built near the well. Muslim traditions connect its construction with Adam and relate that Abraham and his son Ishmael rebuilt it. This is the Ka'ba, the holiest shrine of Islam. Mecca attracted both 5 worshippers and traders, and its position on a main trading route meant it enjoyed considerable prosperity. Until the seventh century C.E. (in the Christian era), Arabs worshipped many gods – one creator of the universe, and a host of minor deities. This changed with the advent of Islam, when the Prophet Muhammad transformed Mecca into one of the greatest pilgrimage centres in the world. 10

Muhammad, the founder of Islam, born in about 570 C.E., was raised by his uncle, Abu Talib. He may have had early contact with Christianity on a trading journey to Syria. Married at twenty-five to Khadijah, a wealthy woman fifteen years his senior, he led a pious life. Later, in his forties, during a period devoted to meditation, he retreated alone to a cave on Mount Hira and spent time in prayer and fasting. Here, 15 in a vision, an angel – whom he believed to be Gabriel – gave him the first verses of the Qur'an, the holy book of Islam. He was told to carry a message to the world that there was only one God, no others.

For three years, he only spoke of his beliefs in private. During this time, he is said to have received the verses of the Qur'an. Once he began to preach, Mecca became 20 very hostile. In 622, Muhammad left for Yathrib (later Medina), narrowly avoiding death; this migration, or *hijra*, was the turning point in his life. Received with zeal, the number of his followers swelled.

In 629, Muhammad approached Mecca with 10,000 men, but met little resistance. His Muslim forces entered the city, casting out the idols that had been previously worshipped 25 and initiating worship of the one God, Allah. The Prophet died in Medina in 632.

All over the world, around 900 million Muslims bow down to face Mecca at five different points during the day – at dawn, midday, afternoon, evening and night. In mosques, its direction is indicated by niches called *mihrabs*. Every year, in the month of *Dhu'l-Hijja* (the twelfth month of the Muslim calendar), pilgrims converge on Mecca from all parts 30 of the world for the *hajj*, the great pilgrimage. All Muslims who possess the means must perform the pilgrimage to Mecca at least once in a lifetime. The city and its surrounding area are considered so sacred that non-Muslims are not admitted. With travel now much easier than in the past, over two million Muslims are able to make the pilgrimage to Mecca each year.

35

adapted from *The Atlas of Holy Places and Sacred Sites*, Colin Wilson

Questions

1.	Why might Mecca have been important to travellers in ancient times?	(2)
2.	In your own words, give two reasons why Mecca 'enjoyed considerable prosperity' (ll.6–7).	(4)
3.	How old was Khadijah when she married? Be careful!	(1)
4.	What was the message Muhammad was given by the angel?	(2)
5.	What was the reaction in Mecca when Muhammad began to preach? Can you) explain why Muhammad's beliefs had such a strong effect?	(5)
6.	What happened when Muhammad arrived in Medina?	(2)
7.	How old was he when he arrived in Mecca with his army?	(1)
8.	Why were the idols cast out?	(2)
9.	How do Muslims in mosques all over the world know which way to face when they bow down to Mecca?	(2)
10.	Explain in your own words what the *hajj* is and who makes it each year.	(4)

Time: 40 minutes   **Total marks available: 25**

Essay

Stories – rather like history – very much depend on who is describing what happened. Two people's versions of the same event may differ wildly.

Tell one of the following stories from two different points of view. Spend about 30 minutes on this.

a) The Burglary

b) The Interview

c) A Family Day Out

(You will see that the titles are the same as for the previous exercise. Choose a different title from the one you chose for that exercise.)

Mr Abney welcomes a guest

Stephen Elliott, an orphan, has been invited by his elderly cousin, Mr Abney, to go to live with him in his grand old house in the country. Mr Abney lives with his housekeeper, Mrs Bunch and his servant, Mr Parkes in Aswarby.

Whatever may have been expected by his neighbours, it is certain that Mr Abney – the tall, the thin, the austere – seemed inclined to give his young cousin a kindly reception. The moment the front door was opened he darted out of his study, rubbing his hands with delight.

'How are you, my boy? – how are you? How old are you?' said he – 'that is, you are not   5
too much tired, I hope, by your journey to eat your supper?'

'No, thank you, sir,' said Stephen, 'I am pretty well.'

'That's a good lad,' said Mr Abney. 'And how old are you, my boy?'

It seemed a little odd that he should have asked the question twice in the first two
minutes of their acquaintance.   10

'I'm twelve years old next birthday, sir,' said Stephen.

'And when is your birthday, my dear boy? Eleventh of September, eh? That's well – that's very well. Nearly a year hence, isn't it? I like – ha, ha! – I like to get these things down in my book. Sure it's twelve? Certain?'

'Yes, quite sure, sir.'   15

'Well, well! Take him to Mrs Bunch's room, Parkes, and let him have his tea – supper – whatever it is.'

'Yes, sir,' answered the staid Mr Parkes and conducted Stephen to the lower regions.

Mrs Bunch was the most comfortable and human person whom Stephen had as yet
met at Aswarby. She made him completely at home; they were great friends in a quarter   20
of an hour: and great friends they remained. Mrs Bunch had been born in the
neighbourhood some fifty-five years before the date of Stephen's arrival, and her
residence at The Hall was of twenty years' standing. Consequently, if anyone knew the
ins and outs of the house and the district, Mrs Bunch knew them and she was by no
means disinclined to communicate her information.   25

Certainly there were plenty of things about The Hall and The Hall gardens which
Stephen, who was of an adventurous and inquiring turn, was anxious to have explained
to him. 'Who built the temple at the end of the laurel walk? Who was the old man
whose picture hung on the staircase, sitting at a table, with a skull under his hand?'
These and many similar points were cleared up by the resources of Mrs Bunch's   30
powerful intellect. There were others, however, of which the explanations furnished
were less satisfactory.

adapted from *Lost Hearts*, MR James

Questions

1. What sort of man does Mr Abney seem to be? Is there anything odd about him?   (4)

2. Did Mr Abney's neighbours expect Stephen to be welcome at The Hall?   (2)

3. How old was Mrs Bunch when Stephen was born? How old was she when she
    arrived at The Hall?   (4)

4. Stephen is 'of an adventurous and inquiring turn', we are told (l.27). Why is Mrs Bunch
    an ideal person for him to talk to?   (3)

5. Can Mrs Bunch answer all his questions adequately? Give a reason for your answer.   (2)

6. MR James is a famous writer of ghost and horror stories. Is there anything in the extract above that suggests this to you? (4)

7. Continue the story for another three or four paragraphs. You do not need to finish it if you don't want to. (6)

Time: 30 minutes   **Total marks available: 25**

Essay

Write on one of the following for 30 minutes:

a) Imagine you are Mr Parkes. Write your diary for the night of Stephen's arrival at Aswarby. Let your imagination go!

b) Stephen gets given his own bedroom at Aswarby. Describe it in detail.

c) The extract refers to 'the old man whose picture hung on the staircase, sitting at a table, with a skull under his hand, (ll.28–29). Tell his story.

Practice paper: Escape from the prison camp

Do this paper in 1 hour 10 minutes. You should spend roughly ten minutes reading the passage and the questions and roughly half an hour answering the questions. The last 30 minutes is for the essay. Try to leave a few minutes for checking.

Joseph is a prisoner. He is kept, chained, in an outdoor prison called 'the cooler'.

On the evening of the third day the guard came as usual. When Joseph heard the soft thud of his footsteps in the snow, he crouched down on the floor at the back of his tiny cell. He had a smooth round stone and a catapult in his hands. He had made the catapult from pine twigs and the elastic sides of his boots. His eyes were fixed on the flap in the door. In a moment the guard would unlock it, peer inside and hand in the food.   5

Tensely, Joseph waited. He heard the key grate in the rusty lock of the outside door of 'the cooler'. The hinges creaked open. There was the sound of a match spluttering – the guard was lighting the lamp. Heavy boots clumped across the floor towards his cell.

Joseph drew back the elastic. He heard the padlock on the flap being unlocked. The flap   10
slid aside.

The guard had not seen Joseph when the stone struck him in the middle of the forehead and knocked him down. The floor shook as he tumbled. He groaned and rolled over.

Joseph must act quickly, before the guard came to his senses. He knew the guard kept   15
his bunch of keys in his greatcoat pocket. He must get hold of them without delay. He must lift the guard till they were within reach.

He took a hook and line from under his bed. He had made the line by cutting thin strips from his blanket and plaiting them together. The hook was a bent four-inch nail that he had smuggled in from his hut.   20

After several attempts, the hook caught in the top fastened button of the guard's greatcoat. He tugged at the line and drew the guard, still groaning, up towards him....higher and higher. Suddenly the line snapped. The guard fell back, striking his head sharply on the floor. The hook was lost.

Joseph had one spare hook, that was all.   25

He tried again. This time the cotton broke and the button went spinning across the floor. He tried for the next button. Again the cotton broke.

He had begun to despair when he saw the keys. They were lying on the floor. They had been shaken out of the greatcoat pocket when the guard fell.

Quickly Joseph fished for the ring of keys and hauled it up. A few moments later he was   30
kneeling beside the senseless body, hastily stripping off the uniform. There was no time to lose. Already the locking-up of the prisoners had started and he could hear the guards shouting at them outside.

Joseph felt warm in the guard's uniform. The greatcoat reached to his ankles. The fur cap had flaps for covering his ears. He smiled to himself as he locked the guard in the   35
freezing cell. Then, turning up his collar so that the tips touched his cheek-bones, he went out into the bitter night.

He walked through the snow towards Block E, where the Hungarian and Rumanian prisoners were kept. In the dark shadows behind the huts he hid until the trumpet sounded the change of guard   40

Hundreds of times he had watched the soldiers of the guard fall in and march out of camp.

He had memorised every order, every movement. It seemed to him quite natural now to be lining up with the others.

"Anything to report?" the officer asked each of them in turn.   45
"All correct, sir," they answered.
"All correct, sir," said Joseph in his best German.
"Guard, dismiss!" said the officer.

Joseph dropped to the rear and followed the other soldiers out – out of the great spiked gate and into freedom. It seemed too good to be true.   50

Some of the soldiers stopped outside the guard-house to gossip. A few went in. Joseph walked straight ahead, turning his head away from the window light as he passed.

"Where are you going?" one of them called.
"Shangri La," he muttered. It was the soldiers' name for the night club in the village where they sometimes spent their off-duty times.   55

Without looking behind him, he walked on.

The Silver Sword, Ian Serraillier

Questions

1. At what time of year did this incident happen? How do you know?   (1)
2. Why does Joseph wait 'tensely' (l.7)?   (1)
3. In paragraph two, Joseph can't see anything but relies on what he can hear to know what is happening. Find three words which tell you what sounds he can hear.   (3)
4. Describe carefully and in detail how Joseph tried to get the keys from the guard.   (4)
5. Why did he strip the guard of his uniform?   (2)
6. How did Joseph know how to behave when lining up with the soldiers?   (2)
7. Was Joseph first through the gate? How do you know?   (2)
8. Why do you think he walked on, 'without looking behind him'?   (2)
9. What sort of a man do you think Joseph is? Back up your answer with evidence from the passage.   (4)
10. How does the writer build up suspense and excitement in this passage? Give as many examples as you can.   (4)

Essay

Answer **ONE** of the following:

a) What do you think happens next? Continue the story from where the passage leaves off.

    or

b) Write a story called 'The Prisoner'.

    or

c) Write a story or a description in which the idea of *disguise* is an important part.

    or

d) Describe a place you found frightening.

Practice paper: Ikey in Orkney

Here is another complete practice paper to be done in 1 hour and a quarter. You have 10 minutes reading time for the comprehension, 30 minutes for the comprehension questions and 30 minutes for the essay. Make sure you save a few minutes for careful checking!

Read through the passage below slowly and carefully. It is in three parts: an introduction; a small story for the month of April; and a second story for the month of June. The events take place on the islands of Orkney, off the north coast of Scotland, and concern a tinker boy called Ikey. 'Tinker' was a word used in Scotland and the Orkneys for travellers.

There was once a tribe of tinkers in Orkney, who went from island to island selling clothespegs and tin mugs and bootlaces. There was a boy called Ikey in this sprawling rootless family. Ikey liked to wander off by himself. He wasn't missed, there were so many laughing fighting sisters and brothers and cousins.

Sometimes the old tinker chief might say, 'Where's that boy Ikey? I haven't seen him for   5
a week or two.' And a tinker wife would reply, 'Ikey's like the moon, he's here and gone again.' A tinker lass would say, 'Ikey's like a wave of the sea, he comes shining among us and then he's nothing but echoes and spray.' The old chief said, 'Ikey is the tinker of the tinkers. He's even an outcast from us vagrants. He's like the wind on the hill…'

April   10

Miss Instone the teacher in Greenvoe village blew her whistle and all the island children – twenty of them – went swirling in through the door of the small school. Ikey looked from the road outside. Miss Instone took the whistle from her mouth and she said, 'You, boy, why aren't you at school? You're the age for school attendance, I know that… Why can't your mother clean you up, you're filthy! Why can't she put a stitch in your   15
rags? Oh, you're a tinker boy, are you… Well all the bairns in my school are neat and washed and shod, however poor they are… I don't want them getting fleas and lice… So you'd better not come in, not today… Still, realise this, you little wretch, you're breaking the law by not attending school. Your parents – if you have any – could be in serious trouble…' Miss Instone went into the classroom and shut the door. 'Slates out!'   20
she shouted. 'Spell the following words…'

On the hillside, a mile further on, Ikey sat on a stone. A little company of early daffodils, in bud still, hung their heads nearby. A small cloud moved over, scattering drops of rain. The green heads twinkled. Then there was a wash of sun across the hill. A lark went up and up into the new patch of blue and was lost, but the sky went on ringing, it seemed   25
even louder, over the hill of Greenvoe.

In the field above, a ewe called anxiously for her lamb, wandering here and there among the rocks and little marshes. (There had been much rain this April.) Then Ikey was aware of a small flutter beside him. It was a lamb like a tiny masker, all black with a white mask for eyes and white forelegs and a white tail. Ikey thought it strange that the   30
very young have no fear, but soon the world is full of shapes of dread. The harlequin lamb nuzzled Ikey's knee. Ikey lifted it and carried it to the ewe. The lark went on stammering out sweetness between two rain clouds. Ikey was on the road, passing the small farm of Cleftbreck. He moved round Cleftbreck in a wide circle, because Rover the dog there had a bad reputation – indeed, once Rover had ripped a rag out of Ikey's   35
trousers, and Ikey hadn't stopped running for a mile, his rags all a-flutter, his breath coming in sobs and gasps…

But Rover must have been out with Berston the farmer at the hill, for there was only Mistress Berston coming in from the henhouse with an aluminium bowl brimming over with eggs. 'Is that you, Ikey?' said the farm wife. 'Hold out your cap. I have more eggs   40 than I know what to do with.' Ikey held out his bonnet and Mistress Berston put six warm eggs into it, three brown and three white. Ikey had never learned to say thank-you but his teeth flashed in his tinker face. He hadn't eaten for two days. He broke an egg with his thumb and emptied it down his throat, then another…

The big cloud that had covered the sun ten minutes before dropped its rain, a lingering prismatic shower. Mistress Berston drew her shawl about her head and scurried indoors. Ikey held his face up to the rain until his hair and his hands were streaming, and his hundred rags clung wetly about him. The sun came out again. Ikey glittered like a fish or a bird. The whole island was clean and sparkling. Ikey broke another egg into his mouth. His throat wobbled. Ikey ran back across the hill. More lambs had been born since he had sat on the stone at lark-rise. As he looked, there was a faint stirring in the cluster of daffodil buds. Slowly, slowly, with a gesture of delight, the first daffodil opened in the wind.

June

The fishermen of Farn village were going down to their boat *Kestrel* one morning when whom should they meet but Merran with the black whisker. No fisherman would dare put to sea, having met Merran. It was a promising fishing day. They sat on their boat and smoked and complained about witches and the evil eye. 'Look!' said Willie the famous creel-maker. 'Here's that tinker boy coming.' Ikey was roaming here and there among the rockpools, looking for sea treasure, a salt-eaten boot or a broken oar. 'An innocent boy like Ikey might cancel a spell,' said Thorfinn, whose hooks were sharper and more barbed than any in Orkney. Ikey refused to go out in the *Kestrel*. 'You don't have to do anything,' said the oldest fisherman, Jeemo. 'Just sit on the thwart and enjoy the sail.' Ikey sat in the stern thwart. The sea got rough beyond Rousay, and Ikey leaned over the stern and spasms of sickness went through him. But the lines came up burgeoning with haddocks, again and again. It was the best morning the Farn men had had fishing all that June. The five baskets amidship were over-brimming with fine fat haddocks.

At last they turned the *Kestrel* for home. Ikey floundered ashore like a dying seal, gray in the face. 'The seasickness never killed anybody,' said the old skipper. 'You'll be as right as rain once you're on the shore road.'

There was a great feast of fish round the tinkers' fire that night. Ikey's appetite was sharper than any seal's. 'I'm never going fishing again,' said Ikey, licking cod juice from his fingers. 'Never.'

From *Winter Tales*, George Mackay Brown

SECTION A (25 MARKS)

1. *In your own words,* say what you learn about the life of the tinkers. (2 marks)

2. Ikey is compared to a number of different things in the passage as a whole. Find three things to which he is compared and list them; then write **one sentence** explaining what these comparisons, taken together, tell us about Ikey. (2 marks)

3. Re-read what Miss Instone says to Ikey. Does she want Ikey to attend her school or not? Give a reason for your answer. (2 marks)

4. What impression does the author want to create when he writes 'a wash of sun' in line 24? (2 marks)

5. When Ikey thinks about the world being full of 'shapes of dread' in line 31, what things might he have in mind? Think about Ikey's life and experiences before you answer and explain why you have chosen the things you mention. (3 marks)

6. Why do you think Mistress Berston gives Ikey the eggs? (2 marks)

7. What do you find interesting about the difference between Mistress Berston's and Ikey's responses to the rain (ll.45–50)? (3 marks)

8. Why do the fishermen want Ikey to go out to sea with them? Give as full an explanation as you can. (3 marks)

9. What kind of boy is Ikey? Write a paragraph about him, mentioning three separate things he does in the passage and explaining what each one tells us about him. (3 marks)

10. Children go to school to learn but they can also learn many things outside school. Write a short paragraph consisting of **no more than three sentences** about the kinds of things children learn outside school. (3 marks)

SECTION B (25 MARKS)

Write an Ikey story for the month of January.

Multiple choice comprehension: Birdsong could beat the winter blues

This is a multiple choice comprehension. Write down the correct letter from the choices you are given. You should take around 20 minutes for this exercise.

Listening to just five minutes of birdsong could be one of the best ways to help get us through the shortest day of the year and give us a much needed boost during the long winter months.

With just under eight hours of daylight, the shortest day of the year in mid-winter is one of the most difficult times of the year for workers – particularly for busy commuters – to experience the beauty of birdsong.

Peter Brash, National Trust ecologist, said:

'Birdsong is one of the most distinctive sounds from the natural world and gives us   5
a warm glow inside when we hear it. We're all attuned to the need to eat five fruit
and vegetables a day or take a 30 minute walk. Taking the time out to listen to five
minutes of birdsong every day could be as beneficial to our well being.'
Whilst some birds can be heard singing most of the year, such as the much loved robin,
for others, including the beautiful song thrush and the garden regulars of the tit family,   10
the period around the shortest day marks the start of their song season.

Mike Dilger, naturalist and TV presenter, added:

'It was birdsong that first drew me into the wonderful world of natural history as I
pondered which birds were singing outside my bedroom window as a child. Hearing
the birds compete for air-time at dawn (and dusk) has to be one of life's greatest joys   15
and for me is still the best way to enhance my least favourite day of the year... And if
I were to put money on it, I'd bet I'll hear the robin first.'

A dawn chorus

There will be more and more species adding to the dawn chorus as the days lengthen in
January and February. Whilst the winter song of the robin is to protect their feeding   20
territory, the song of birds such as song thrush and great tit indicates that their thoughts
are turning to summer, marking out breeding territories and finding mates. The first
bird song is a reminder that the days are lengthening and whilst it may be the depth
of winter, spring is just around the corner. The peak time of the year for birdsong is
the spring with the dawn chorus in May but there are still a great variety of birds to   25
be heard even on the 21 December.

abridged and adapted from *National Trust News*, December 2010

1. 'Busy commuters' find it hard to hear birdsong because:

   a) they are working so hard b) the birds are hibernating

   c) they are travelling when the birds are singing d) the days are too short

2. Which bird sings all year round?

   a) the tit b) the song thrush c) the robin d) the wren

3. Peter Brash refers to 'the need to eat five fruit and vegetables a day or take a 30 minute walk' (ll.6–7). What does he suggest is equally important for our health?

   a) listening to five minutes of birdsong b) getting up early c) gardening d) keeping warm

4. When Mike Dilger writes of the birds who 'compete for air-time at dawn (and dusk)' (l.15) he is suggesting that they:

   a) can be heard on the radio b) fight each other c) only sing in the morning and evening

   d) are all singing at the same time in the mornings and evenings

5. 'enhance' (l.16) means to:

   a) shorten b) make better c) lengthen d) make louder

6. The 'dawn chorus' (l.19) is:

   a) the number of birds in winter b) noise made by people going to work

   c) a song sung by commuters d) birdsong in the early morning

7. 'breeding territories' (l.22) means:

   a) areas in the sun b) farming areas c) places where birds sing

   d) places where they can nest and lay eggs

8. Birdsong is not just there to give pleasure to humans. It also:

   a) entertains other birds b) marks out breeding or feeding territory and attracts mates

   c) shows that it is winter d) is healthy for them

9. You can hear most birdsong:

   a) on December 21st b) in May in early morning c) on short days d) in the garden

You may feel you will need more practice in this type of format. Your teacher may be able to supply more multiple choice papers for you to practise with.

ANSWERS

Some of the **questions** do not require answers to be given here – either because there is no right/wrong answer or because the exercises merely require practice and the answers should be obvious. However, you will find answers below to any exercises where right/wrong is appropriate.

1 THE RULES OF WRITING

SPELLING

Common spelling confusions

Adding 'd' or -ed

page 7

joked	flattered	sniffed
climbed	hurried	smiled
thrilled	surprised	tramped
tamed	spotted	battled
adopted	snapped	spied
cuddled	liked	acted

page 7

Sarah and Laura *poured* the popcorn into a bowl and *started* to munch.
Karim and Naveen *cycled* to the park and *waved* to some friends.
Mrs Chinwicket *stirred* the pot after she *skinned* the slippery snake.
Mr Morpish *married* Miss Chirping after they *learned/learnt* to dance at an evening class.
Laura *copied* Karim's homework but Mrs Chinwicket *spotted* it.

Double letters

page 8

tripping/tripped
strapping/strapped
slipping/slipped
slimming/slimmed
flopping/flopped
skipping/skipped
batting/batted
thinning/thinned

page 8

Sarah and Laura *chopped* firewood for the bonfire and *dropped* a lighted match to start it off.
Mr Morpish *scrapped* his car last week.
Julia *scarred* herself with the rusty nail.

Word games

page 10

salad	pasta
pizza	chips
sausage	curry
cereal	bacon
cheese	sandwich

page 10

Animals	Colours	English towns	Football clubs
monkey	blue	Brighton	Spurs
tiger	orange	London	Arsenal
lion	violet	Leeds	Chelsea
giraffe	scarlet	York	West Ham
elephant	brown	Durham	Liverpool
crocodile	navy	Coventry	Aston Villa
rabbit	green	Dover	Bolton
sheep	white	Lincoln	Leeds
wolf	grey	Norwich	Fulham
buffalo	yellow	Bristol	Blackburn

Commas

page 12

Sarah has been going to ballet for years. Every Thursday, since she was four, has been ballet class. Now she is bored and wants to try something else. Her friend, Laura, is a brownie but Sarah doesn't want to be a brownie. Karim does gymnastics but Sarah thinks she's no good at gym. Naveen isn't sporty at all.

One day, Sarah has a new idea and tells her mother she wants to try judo. Her mother, thinking this an excellent idea, rushes out to buy a leotard. Sarah knows you need a special suit for judo. They take the leotard back and come home with a judo kit.

page 12

We live in Ealing, part of London in the south east, so we live in England but we also live in Great Britain, the British Isles and in the United Kingdom. It's a bit complicated. We're also part of Europe, the British Commonwealth (which used to be the Empire) and we also live in the northern hemisphere. Sometimes it's said that we live in the West but I don't understand this. We might be west of Europe but we are east of the United States so it doesn't mean anything. It all depends on where you are.

page 12

Naveen, a thoughtful boy, really likes computers. He also likes dinosaurs and modern reptiles but his best friend, a boy called Karim, is more interested in football and other sports. He is always trying to get Naveen, who hates sport, to go to a match with him but Naveen, who dislikes noisy crowds, prefers to spend a Saturday afternoon on his computer with his other friends, Luke, Simon, Sahib and Vijay.

Punctuating speech

Punctuation inside speech marks

page 13

'Mr Sloppy's ice cream is,' declared Sarah, 'the best in the world.'

'Rubbish!' replied Naveen, rudely. 'My mum's is loads better. It's made from real fruit.'

'So what?' said Sarah. 'Mr Sloppy's couldn't be better.'

'Let's see,' said Naveen. 'Why don't we test them both on Karim and Laura and see who's right?'

'I'm right. You'll see,' retorted Sarah. 'Nobody's better than Mr Sloppy and I should know because he's my dad.'

'Where's my jacket?' yelled Karim's sister, Shireen, from her room. 'I'm late at the stables and it's my turn to do the horses' food. They'll be starving!'

'It's probably under your bed where I found your T-shirt, socks, sweatshirt and most of your underwear,' replied her overworked Mum.

'Thanks, Mum,' shouted Shireen, 'but I can't find my jodhpurs.'

'That's the second pair this term,' sighed her Mum, despairingly.

'I can't help it,' responded Shireen. 'Jodhpurs aren't cool anyway and, Mum, don't get a shock when you come in, but I've had my head shaved.'

In the shops, Naveen met his friend Karim. Karim was with his mum who is a friend of Naveen's mum. The mums started talking. At first, Naveen and Karim did not mind. Then they got bored and Karim, who can be rather wild, had an idea.

'I am going to pile up all the cans of baked beans,' he said, 'and I dare you to do it with the spaghetti hoops.'

When the towers were higher than Karim and Naveen and about to topple over, a shop assistant noticed what the boys had done. The manager came over to the mums.

'Are these two boys with you?' he enquired.

'Watch out!' cried Naveen. 'The beans are falling over!'

'Look at my cat,' said Laura, 'she's got things crawling on her fur.'

'Ugh!' screamed Laura's mother. 'What's the matter with her? It's disgusting! What is it?'

'I've no idea,' mumbled Laura's dad from behind his son's Rice Krispies packet.

'Who cares anyway?' sneered Laura's brother, Paul, a very tiresome boy. 'Cats stink. It's probably got fleas. My friend's sister's cat had fleas the size of gerbils.'

Apostrophes

Possession

page 16

the homework of Sarah – Sarah's homework
the gym of the school – the school's gym
the cages of the animals – the animals' cages
the staff room of the teachers – the teachers' staff room
the job of Mrs Watson – Mrs Watson's job
the car of Mr Das – Mr Das's car
the picnic of the families – the families' picnic
the ideas of the professors – the professors' ideas
the speech of the president – the president's speech
the homes of the millionaire – the millionaire's homes
the club of the men – the men's club
the T-shirt of Thomas – Thomas's T-shirt

page 16

'*What's* the point of going to *Naveen's* house if *I'm* not allowed to play in his tree house?' complained Karim. '*Naveen's dad's* brilliant. *He's* made this amazing tree house. *It's* got all kinds of gadgets and doors and clever things like windows that really open and a ladder that unfolds on its own. *We're* really boring in this family and *there's* nothing to do and *dad's* no good at making things. *Ben's* going to help his dad make a table. *They've* got brilliant tools in their shed. Anyway, the tree house is really safe and it's the best tree house I've ever seen and I will be fine with Naveen's dad there, so, please, Mum, say *you'll* let me go!'

Three tips on apostrophes

page 16

The dog wags *its* tail
It's my dog
My car has lost *its* bumper
The spider made *its* web
It's a lovely day
My cat has lost *its* collar
I think *it's* going to rain
I'm afraid *it's* broken!
Do you know *its* name?

page 17

'Where's *your* rucksack? You've left *your* socks in it and they need washing.'

'*It's* in the car. I'll get it. *It's* a bit muddy. I dropped it on the pitch and it also broke *its* zip when I was running for the bus. Everything fell out. I might have lost *your* phone too. I think it just slipped out of *its* case.'

'I hope *you're* having me on! *You're* in big trouble if *you're* not! After you lost *your* phone you promised to be more careful!'

'*It's* not really my fault. I've been telling you about the zip for ages. The phone was useless anyway. *It's* lost *its* memory.'

'Well, *it's* not the only one, is it? *You're* a fine one to talk!'

Parts of speech

Adverbs

page 19

The banana was brought in on a lordly dish. My grandfather peeled it with a golden knife.
   .... - - - - - - - -   *//////* .... - - - -   */////////* ....
He then cut a sliver off and, with a golden fork, put it in his mouth and carefully tasted it.
  ~~~ - - - ....   *////////* ...... - - -   *////* ....   ~~~~~ - - - -

Avoiding common mistakes

They're, there or their

page 21

Where are the boys? *They're* looking for *their* football. It went somewhere over *there* in the bushes. *They're* probably crawling about on *their* hands and knees getting *their* trousers muddy. It's nearly dark now so *there* isn't much point carrying on looking. *They're* probably just enjoying getting dirty!

Wear, where, were or we're

page 21

We're going to have a party. *We're* both going to be eleven and Sarah and I *were* discussing it all through lunch with our friends. The two problems are *where* to have it and what to *wear*. I'd like to have it in the hall *where* the disco was, as the lights *were* brilliant at Karim's party. *We're* having a meeting to discuss it later. We *were* going to meet at Sarah's house as that is *where* I left the shoes I want to *wear* but she can't find them. Do you know *where* your high-heeled shoes are so that I can paint them yellow?

Practice or practise, etc

page 22

After football *practice* at school, Naveen rushes home to *practise* his ball skills. Ali, his father, has *devised* a programme to help him and tries to *advise* him but Naveen doesn't want his dad's *advice*. He prefers to watch his Premiership video and get all the *advice* he wants from that. 'I get loads of *practice* at school,' he tells his dad, 'and loads of *advice* from my teacher, too!'

'Ah!' said Ali. 'But I *prophesy* that you will do much better if you *practise* my programme. I have *devised* it specially for you! And I've just got my coaching *licence*!'

Effect or affect

page 22

'I don't think that late nights have a good *effect* on your concentration,' said Sarah's mother after Sarah had fallen asleep over her homework.

'It's not the late nights that *affect* me,' replied Sarah. 'It's the *effect* of having to get up early in the mornings!'

'An understandable *effect*,' remarked her father, 'for someone who reads in bed until 3.00am! How can you not expect so little sleep to *affect* how you feel the next day?'

'Oh Sarah!' sighed her mother. 'What *effect* will that have on your gym display today?'

Choose or chose; lose or loose

page 23

Will you help me *choose* a new hair slide? The clasp on my old one has become *loose* and I need to get a new one as I'm bound to *lose* this one before long! It keeps falling off. My gran *chose* one for me last week but it was pink, and I hate pink. I can't believe she *chose* it. I might even try to *lose* it.

To or too

page 23

'We're going *to* have a picnic. Do you want *to* come *too*?'

'Not much. What's there *to* do on a picnic? Anyway, I'm *too* tired and it's *too* wet. It's probably going *to* rain again, *too*!'

'What a misery you are! Aren't you going *to* do anything today? Do come! I'm going *to* make a lovely picnic. Sarah and Laura are coming *too* and we may go *to* the pond *to* hire a boat.'

'Oh all right! But I won't do anything *too* energetic. And I want *to* eat a lot. Understand?'

'*Too* right! You always do!'

Properly or probably; Uninterested or disinterested

page 24

'We'll *probably* go to the museum tomorrow,' Rajiv's mum told him. 'I really want you to look *properly* at those dinosaurs so you can get down to your project.'

'I can do the project from the internet,' argued Rajiv. 'I am completely *uninterested* in dinosaurs and I'd rather play with Karim.'

'Well, Karim's mum said she and Karim would come too,' replied his mum, 'which is kind and totally *disinterested* on their part as Karim's project is on engines.'

'Now I'm *properly* confused,' complained Rajiv. 'Karim said he would *probably* be at his dad's office tomorrow.'

'He *probably* changed his mind,' said Rajiv's mum.

Except or accept

page 25

Everyone *except* Naveen came to Karim's party. His mother had telephoned to *accept* the invitation but he didn't turn up. Karim refused to start the game without him. 'No-one *except* Naveen understands how to play,' he complained.

'I can't *accept* that,' said Tom. 'I can read the instructions and teach everyone else.'

'That would be fine,' said Karim, '*except* that you're holding them upside down.'

'Let's have tea,' suggested his mum. 'Naveen did *accept* your invitation so I'm sure he's on his way.'

'OK,' said Karim, 'we can eat everything *except* the salt and vinegar crisps because they're Naveen's favourite.'

Fewer or less

page 25

Laura decided to invite her four best friends to dinner rather than have a birthday party this year. Her mother was pleased. '*Fewer* friends means *less* mess,' she said.

'*Fewer* friends means *fewer* presents too,' replied Laura, ruefully.

'*Less* spilled drink, *fewer* sausages trodden into the carpet, *fewer* crisp crumbs under the table, *less* waste paper and *fewer* tears when people don't win all the games. Sounds good to me,' mused Laura's mother.

'And *less* fun too,' thought Laura, beginning to change her mind.

Compliment or complement

page 26

Judge Grumpus met Mrs Chinwicket at the station. 'May I say,' he whispered in her ear, 'how utterly charming you look today?' She beamed at this unexpected *compliment*. 'And,' he continued, dribbling slightly, 'that your green scarf is the perfect *complement* to your extraordinary complexion. A quite remarkable colour match!' Mrs Chinwicket felt she should *compliment* Judge Grumpus in return, only it was hard to know what to say. The colour of his brown tie was not *complemented* by the custard stains down his front and the cat hairs around his bristly chin made it hard to *compliment* his appearance in general.

Should've; could've; would've; might've

page 27

'I can't find my homework book,' said Karim.

'Did you leave it at school?' asked his mum, while she was putting the shopping away.

'I *could have*,' admitted Karim, 'but it *would have* been on the top of my desk and I *would have* seen it when I was packing my bag.'

'Well, you *should have* been more careful,' said Karim's mum. 'I *should have* thought you *would have* learned to remember important things by now.'

'I suppose I *could have* dropped it somewhere,' Karim wondered. 'Oh well, I'll have my burger now and I'll ring Naveen about the homework afterwards.'

'Burgers!' exclaimed his mother. 'I knew I'd forgotten something!'

'Hm,' muttered Karim. 'I *should have* thought you *would have* learned to remember important things by now.'

'I can't find my homework book,' said Karim.

'Did you leave it at school?' asked his mum, while she was putting the shopping away.

'I *could've*,' admitted Karim, 'but it *would've* been on the top of my desk and I *would've* seen it when I was packing my bag.'

'Well, you *should've* been more careful,' said Karim's mum. 'I *should've* thought you *would've* learned to remember important things by now.'

'I suppose I *could've* dropped it somewhere,' Karim wondered. 'Oh well, I'll have my burger now and I'll ring Naveen about the homework afterwards.'

'Burgers!' exclaimed his mother. 'I knew I'd forgotten something!'

'Hm,' muttered Karim. 'I *should've* thought you *would've* learned to remember important things by now.'

Me or I

page 27

Rajiv gave presents to Karim and *me*. Laura gave sweets to Sarah and *me*. I gave the books to Karim, and Laura and *I* gave the game to Rajiv. When Karim and *I* opened our presents, I was surprised as Rajiv had given Laura and *me* exactly what we had given him!

page 28

Mrs Chinwicket called *Laura and me* to her desk and she was clearly cross with us. *Laura and I* had just been sitting in the playground and couldn't think of any reason that we might be in trouble. Mrs Chinwicket looked sternly at *Laura and me* and snarled. 'What have you to say for yourselves?' she demanded. I tried to speak but my voice sounded very small.

'What have *Laura and I* done?' I asked.

e.g. or i.e.

page 28

I'm having a party really soon *i.e.* on Saturday and I've got loads to get ready, *e.g.* the food, the drinks, clearing the room and something to wear. My best friend, *i.e.* Sarah, is coming to help and she's bringing quite a lot of stuff, *e.g.* balloons, decorations, some of the food and so on. I'm a bit worried about one thing *i.e.* the weather, as I really want to be outside but there's nothing I can do about that. With luck, the main event, *i.e.* the fireworks, will be fine.

2 IMPROVING YOUR WRITING SKILLS

WRITING INTERESTINGLY

Focus on the vocabulary

page 37

Words that you could substitute for 'said' – there are about 100 in the list, but you could find at least as many more.

acknowledged	allowed	announced
answered	barked	bawled
bayed	bellowed	blasted
brayed	breathed	cackled
called	carped	cawed
cheeped	chirped	chirruped
chortled	chuckled	claimed
complained	coughed	cried
decided	declared	demanded
exclaimed	explained	gasped
granted	grimaced	groused
growled	grumbled	grunted
hinted	hissed	hooted

howled	insisted	interrupted
joked	laughed	lisped
moaned	mumbled	munched
murmured	muttered	neighed
niggled	queried	questioned
persevered	persisted	pleaded
proclaimed	protested	purred
rallied	ranted	rasped
rejoined	replied	reported
responded	retorted	roared
scolded	screamed	shouted
shrieked	sighed	smiled
smirked	snarled	sniffed
snorted	sobbed	spat
stammered	stormed	stuttered
suggested	tittered	trilled
triumphed	trumpeted	ventured
volunteered	wept	wheezed
whimpered	whined	whinged
whinnied	whispered	whistled
yelled	yelped	

page 37

Words that you could substitute for 'went' – there are about 100 in the list, but you could find at least as many more.

advanced	ambled	barged
beetled	belted	bobbed
bounced	cantered	capered
careered	charged	chugged
climbed	clumped	continued
crawled	crept	danced
darted	dawdled	disappeared
dodged	dragged	drifted
escaped	fled	flew
galloped	hared	hiked
hopped	idled	jogged
journeyed	limped	loitered
loped	lumbered	marched
meandered	moved	paced
padded	paraded	plodded
plunged	pottered	pranced
proceeded	processed	prowled
raced	ran	roved
sauntered	scampered	scarpered
scrambled	shuffled	sidled
skipped	skulked	slipped
slithered	slunk	sneaked
sped	splashed	sprinted
staggered	stalked	stamped
started	steamed	stormed
strayed	strolled	stumbled
swaggered	swayed	tacked

tiptoed	trailed	toddled
traipsed	tramped	travelled
tripped	trotted	trudged
trundled	vanished	vaulted
waddled	waded	walked
wandered		

3 THE EXAM

ESSAYS

Descriptions

page 48

simile: like the painted face of a savage

metaphor: It was a town of machinery and tall chimneys, out of which interminable serpents of smoke trailed themselves for ever and ever, and never got uncoiled.

simile: like the head of an elephant in a state of melancholy madness

EXAM PRACTICE

The answers given to the **comprehension questions** are suggestions. Obviously, the content must be correct but wording will, of course, vary. Some questions have no right/wrong answers but the responses need to be sensible and show evidence of careful reading and understanding in each case.

Pinched Legs!

page 56

1. *Emil is on a train,* is quite sufficient. (2)

2. *He jumped because he had nearly fallen asleep and didn't want to,* is sufficient. (2)

3. *He didn't want to be alone with 'Bowler-hat,'* is sufficient. (2)

4. This question needs both its parts answered. *No, Emil doesn't enjoy History lessons. I know this because he finds himself falling asleep during them.* (3)

5. *He refused to fight Pony because, as she weighed less than him, it would have been unfair,* will do, but, as the question asks, 'why do you think...?' it would not be wrong – though hardly politically correct! – to add a comment about her being a girl or suggesting that Emil felt he was much too powerful for her. (3)

6. *He pinches his legs and he counts buttons on the seat.* (2)

7. There are no right or wrong answers here – anything intelligent and imaginative in the context would gain marks. (4)

8. The only danger here is in not obeying instructions, especially the *either/or* nature of the question. (7)

Banana Man

page 57

1. *The gardener was sent to Kew,* is sufficient. (1)

2. *He had heard that bananas taste better straight from the tree,* is sufficient. (2)

3. A good answer will deal with both parts of the question. How? *Lord Leconfield could have asked the gardener for regular reports on the tree's progress. He might have visited the tree to see for himself how it was doing.* Why? *He would have done this because he was eager to taste the banana and was impatient to know when he could.* (3)

4. *The onlookers were full of excitement and no-one dared say anything. Everyone watched in suspense etc.* The question is worth only 3 marks so much more is unnecessary unless there is time to spare. (3)

5. *He flung the dish, the banana and his cutlery onto the floor in a rage, exclaiming that the banana tasted 'just like any damn banana.' –* or something close to this. (3)

6. A good answer to this – given the number of available marks – will talk of the training of the gardener, the expensive building of the special greenhouse, the length of time the tree would have taken to grow and the final, wasteful destruction of it all. (3)

7. Any reasonable equivalents that would make sense in the context would be acceptable here, a) *equipment, tools and necessary materials* (2) b) *bore fruit, produced a banana* (2) c) *grand, magnificent, richly ornate,* etc. (2)

8. Again, for 4 marks, this should be fairly detailed. Examiners would look for evidence of reading between the lines, *he is extravagant, given to sudden enthusiasms and wild ideas, unreasonable and bad-tempered, even childish,* and so on. (4)

Gathering Leaves

pages 58–59

1. *The writer is collecting fallen leaves. He is using a spade and bags.* (2)

2. *He is comparing the rustling noise he makes collecting the dry leaves with the noise of rabbits and deer running away.* (2)

3. *He is trying to collect leaves with a spade but it is hard to pick them up that way as they just fall off.* (2)

4. *'Light as balloons' and 'Like rabbit and deer/Running away' are similes; mountains is a metaphor.* (2)

5. *He's trying to pick up the leaves in his arms but they don't stay in his arms and go all over the place.* (2)

6. *The leaves are useless, weightless and colourless so he wonders why he is bothering collecting them.* (3)

7. This is an open question and there is no right answer. Anything that suggests that collecting something that has grown and lived its life is worth doing is worth a point or two. There is also a sense that the activity in itself may be worth something. (3)

8. *He is hard-working, he rather resents the job but carries on, even a little amused by it and by the fact that he is doing it. He is a thinking man who asks questions about what he is doing and why. His language is straightforward and easy to understand even if the questions he asks are hard to grasp – like the leaves!* (3)

9. Again – an open question. This requires detail, imaginative description and sticking to the title. (6)

Buffalo Halt

pages 59–60

1. *They are in comfortable seats in their railway carriage/train.* 'In a train,' on its own is insufficient. (2)

2. The skill here is in describing how a seated passenger sees what is passing on a train journey by looking through the window. This needs to be well described to gain full marks. (3)

3. *The buffalo pass across the railway line in a huge crowd, row on row, and block the line so that the train can't continue on its journey.* (2)

4. *It is impossible to stop or divert a herd of buffalo once it has started off.* (2)

5. Something that explains that *Mr Fogg was very pressed for time and would not have wanted this delay but that he seems very calm.* (3)

6. *Passepartout seems to be an impatient and excitable person who would be happy to shoot at the buffalo and who is not prepared to make allowances for different customs in a foreign country. He is quick to criticise others and doesn't think through the consequences of his suggestions.* (3)

7. *As it would have been impossible to divert the herd and as he would probably just have damaged and even derailed his train, the driver did the right thing in just waiting till the herd had passed by.* (3)

8. *The driver could go faster than planned (accelerate) to make up some of the time.* (2)

9. This requires an understanding of the immensity of the herd and of the fact that it stretches from immediately in front of the train to way off on the horizon. The answer should also refer to the fact that it was nightfall. (5)

Life on Earth

pages 61–62

1. The two crucial points here are that the answer must come from the first paragraph, as stipulated, and that it should mention the three 'empty' areas – the land, the sky and the sea. (3)

2. The answer is in two parts: a) *no, the world wasn't empty* and b) *I know this because the second paragraph gives examples of the various animals which could be found.* (2)

3. *Mammals developed in new ways,* is sufficient. (2)

4. One mark for each diet: *leaves, meat, insects.* (3)

5. *They lived on open ground,* is sufficient. (2)

6. *They ate insects.* (2)

7. Any four from a) *they were large* b) *they ate plants* c) *they were mammals* d) *they had horns* e) *they looked like rhinoceroses* f) *they lived on open ground.* (4)

8. *Triassic, Cretaceous, Tertiary.* (3)

9. *mouse, rat, cat, horse, bat, terrier, monkey, ape, human, rabbit, elephant, camel, dog, bear, pig, beaver, camel, brontothere, rhinoceros.* (4, 1 mark for each 4 named)

She lies by the Island of Spices and Zephyrs

pages 62–63

1. *The 'she' is the wrecked ship.* (1)

2. a) *The atmosphere is peaceful, relaxed, carefree and happy.* (2)

   b) Most people would say 'yes' to this and refer to the climate, the relaxed and peaceful atmosphere, the playfulness of the natural world and the beauty of the place. If a child says they would *not* like to visit, this is not, of course, wrong but they need to justify what they say, e.g. *I prefer the bustle of city life* or *I would find it boring not to have lots to do!* (2)

3. You could make a case for the monkeys, the gold fish, the cloud and the sea weeds – human feelings or behaviour are attributed to them all. (2)

4. Any of the examples in all four of the verses, e.g. the monkeys, the humming birds, the gold fish, the cloud, the roses would do. The marks will be earned by an answer demonstrating a responsive reading and pleasure in the imaginative pictures created by the poet. (3)

5. The explanation is that the ship was wrecked on a rock and the question is whether anyone knows the full story of what happened. (4)

6. An opportunity for an imaginative response to the poem. A good answer will pick up on the detail and the suggestions in the poem while being a real creative piece, making imaginative use of the setting and the mystery. (6)

Costume Drama

pages 63–64

1. *Two from – The family went to swim, to sun-bathe, to have a picnic.* (2)
2. *This was when mother removed her housecoat to reveal her costume.* (2)
3. *Roger thought Mother was being attacked by a sea monster and he wanted to defend her.* (2)
4. *The costume was large and very impressive. It seems to have been made of very thick material, was baggy, and had a lot of frills and fluttery, extra bits of material attached to it.* (3)
5. *It expanded and took in a lot of air, blowing up like a balloon.* (2)
6. *No one was able to help Mother for so long because they were laughing too much.* (2)
7. This is a subtle question as Larry is only referred to twice and each time as having made a clever and rather intellectual remark. So, any answer which says that Larry seems clever and to like words and imaginative comparisons would deserve full marks. (2)
8. A good answer to this question as from mother's point of view would, first of all, include the various stages of the incident, *the display of the costume and entering the cold water, the attack by Roger, the sitting down, Theodore's rescue and so on.* It would also omit the unflattering descriptions of the costume. For full marks it would have to convey what it felt like to be Mother undergoing this experience – perhaps even the frustration with her unsympathetic family. The story from Roger's point of view would involve his sense of fear and outrage that mother was being attacked by the sea monster, a full description of his bravery in rescuing her and, possibly, some sense of hurt that his efforts were not appreciated. (5)
9. This is clearly an individual and subjective question. For full marks, there would need to be a real engagement with the passage and a use of it in detail to convey your feelings. For example – *I like the bit when the costume gets blown up as I can really imagine what this looks like...* or *I think the writer creates very believable characters in just a short passage.* It is, of course, possible that you don't like the passage, in which case this point of view should be supported by detailed reference to the passage. (5)

NB This is an excellent exercise to ensure careful reading. Those who do not realise that Roger is the family dog will come seriously unstuck. There are plenty of words, e.g. 'barking' and 'growling', that give clear clues.

Mecca

pages 64–65

1. *Mecca might have been important because of the well* is sufficient. (2)
2. *Mecca attracted worshippers to the shrine as well as lots of traders. All these visitors would have helped to make it prosperous.* (4)
3. *Khadijah was 40 when she married.* (1)
4. *The angel told Muhammad that there was only one God.* (2)
5. *The reaction in Mecca when Muhammad began to preach was hostile/angry/cross/worried. This was because he wanted to change the religion and stop people worshipping the gods they were used to and turn to one single God* – something that gets across these facts is necessary here. (5)
6. *People were very enthusiastic about him and he got many more followers.* This is a hard question because of the vocabulary involved. (2)
7. *He was about 59.* (1)
8. *The idols were cast out because Muhammad and his followers wanted people to worship only one God and not lots of gods and idols.* (2)

9. *Muslims who want to face Mecca know which way to turn when they are in mosques because there are niches called mihrabs, which show the right direction.* This is not easy to explain and credit should be given for understanding the idea even if the expression isn't perfect. (2)

10. *The hajj is a great pilgrimage which all Muslims who can should make at least once in their lives. Two million manage it each year.* (4)

Mr Abney welcomes a guest

pages 66–67

1. *Mr Abney is clearly strange and unused to children. He is tall, thin and austere (rather stern and remote) yet he seems thrilled to see Stephen – though 'rubbing his hands with delight' sounds a bit over-enthusiastic. His asking Stephen how old he is twice is also odd – why is he asking? – and his enjoyment of the actual date of Stephen's birthday is also odd. His home in the large old house is also somewhat unusual and unsettling.* (4)

2. *The first sentence suggests that his neighbours did not expect Mr Abney to welcome Stephen.* (2)

3. *Mrs Bunch was 44. She arrived at The Hall at 35 years old.* (4)

4. *Mrs Bunch is an ideal person for Stephen to talk to because he has lots of questions and Mrs Bunch a) is very well informed about The Hall and the neighbourhood and b) likes talking.* (3)

5. *The last two sentences suggest that there are some things that Mrs Bunch can't – or won't talk about.* (2)

6. This is an open question in that there is no right/wrong answer but there are plenty of clues in the somewhat creepy setting of the story, the unanswered questions, Mr Abney's oddness and unlikely friendliness towards Stephen, etc. (4)

7. A good answer will maintain the mystery and develop the story by picking up details from the passage and trying to write in a similar style. (6)

Escape from the prison camp

pages 68–69

1. *It happens in the winter. I know because Joseph hears the guard's footsteps in the snow.* Both parts of the answer are needed for the marks. (1)

2. *He waits tensely because he is nervous and anxious, he doesn't know how things will turn out and because it is so important.* A good answer will convey this mix. (1)

3. Any words not from paragraph two will be discounted. Any three from these are acceptable: *grate, creaked, spluttering, clumped.* Only 3 marks are available. (3)

4. *Joseph used a catapult made of boot elastic and pine twigs to shoot a smooth round stone onto the forehead of the guard. This knocked him out. The guard kept the keys in his pocket. As the guard was lying there, Joseph dropped a hook on a line and tried to hook it into the guard's button to draw him up to where he could reach the pocket. However, the line broke once and the cotton on the guard's buttons broke twice and each time the guard fell back to the floor.* A good answer will use all this information. This amount of detail and clarity is necessary for full marks. (4)

5. *Joseph needed to wear the uniform as a disguise so that soldiers would think he was one of them. It also kept him warm.* The first point is the one needed for the marks. (2)

6. *He had seen the soldiers marching, lining up and obeying orders so often that he knew it all by heart and it was easy for him to do as they did.* (2)

7. *Joseph drops 'to the rear' and 'followed' the other soldiers, which shows that he was not first through the gate.* (2)

8. *Joseph doesn't look behind him partly because he wants to look confident and partly because he doesn't want to risk being recognised.* This is the obvious answer but the question allows for other plausible responses. (2)

9. This is an opportunity to read between the lines. Full marks go to an answer which conveys Joseph's foresight and resourcefulness (pine twigs, boot elastic, nail), his physical strength (lifting the guard), his tenacity, patience, bravery and nerve under stress – the whole episode. Some children may see him in a negative way – he is in prison so he must be bad, he hurts the guard and so on. However, best answers will refer to the passage as evidence of the characteristics they identify. At least three sentences will be needed here. (4)

10. The best answers will write in detail about Joseph's tense wait, the protracted efforts to get the keys and the 'will he/won't he be caught' nature of the end of the passage. (4)

Essay

With the story questions a), b) and c), high marks will go to a well-thought-out piece which is relevant to the title and reaches a plausible conclusion. a) needs to be a careful continuation written, as far as possible, in the same style as the passage and writing about Joseph in a way that is consistent with the passage. b) and c) are challenging as no further suggestions are given and the piece needs to hold together as a narrative in the time given. Marks should be awarded for the quality of the imagination and the writing and for the plausibility of the narrative. d) is a description though many will turn it into a narrative. This would not prohibit the giving of high marks but description must be the main purpose of the piece.

Ikey in Orkney

pages 70–72

1. There is a great deal of information and marks can be given for any of the following points. *The tinkers are a travelling people with no fixed home. They are a huge family in which no-one takes particular trouble over supervising the children so Ikey is not missed if he goes off on his own. They live by selling household items. They are poor and poorly dressed. They live alongside but not really with the Orkney people.* NB the question does not ask for *judgements* about the life of the tinkers. (2)

2. *He is compared to: the moon, a wave of the sea, the wind on the hill, a fish, a bird, a dying seal. All these comparisons show how much part of the natural world and its creatures Ikey is.* (2)

3. There is no right or wrong answer to this one. She is clearly in two minds – on the one hand feeling that all children should be in school, on the other hand, not wanting her nice clean children contaminated by the filthy tinker boy. Any answer that conveys this would deserve marks. On balance, Miss Instone would probably prefer Ikey to be in school rather than not. (2)

4. *The phrase conveys a sense of a faint sunlight, reflecting the wetness of the rainfall, as in a watercolour picture.* (2)

5. *'Shapes of dread' conveys a sense of all that threatens life – homelessness, predators, hunger, hostility from those who share the outside space, harsh weather etc.* A good answer will explain that these are things which Ikey knows well from his life so far and his family's experience and he knows how dangerous they can be. (3)

6. *She knows Ikey and has some sense of how he lives and how he has no regular food. She is clearly a generous person who feels some interest in and sympathy for Ikey.* (2)

7. *Mistress Berston has a house-dweller's response to the rain and hurries to get out of it. She has no wish to get wet. Ikey is entirely used to being wet and living in the outdoors so he does not think of trying to avoid or escape it. He almost seems to relish it.* (3)

8. *The fishermen are superstitious people and seeing Merran is regarded as being bad luck and likely to bring danger at sea. However, it was a good day for fishing for other reasons so they wanted to go. They look for a way of somehow getting round the evil of seeing Merran and, whereas on other occasions, Ikey might not be a welcome arrival, now they find reasons – his innocence – why Ikey* *might counteract the threat posed by Merran. So they want to take Ikey with them to bring them good luck and protect them from bad luck.* (3)

9. The answer needs to bring out his mix of independence from his tribe and his dependence on the natural world and the Orkney people. It should show how much part of the landscape he is but how he is aware of its threats and dangers. He has fears and vulnerability as well as strength. (3)

10. Any thoughtful and well-written answer should be well rewarded. As the rubric is specific about only three sentences, one mark should be docked if more is written. (3)

Birdsong could beat the winter blues

pages 72–73

1. c
2. c
3. a
4. d
5. b
6. d
7. d
8. b
9. b

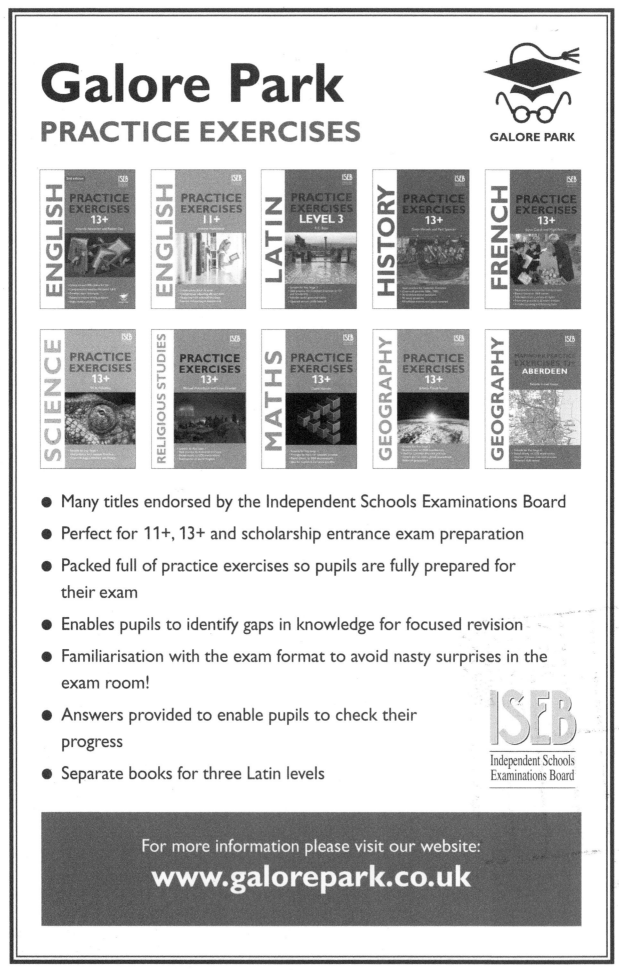